You Owe You

ALSO BY ERIC THOMAS

The Secret to Success
Greatness Is Upon You
Average Skill Phenomenal Will

You Owe You

Ignite Your Power, Your Purpose, and Your Why

Eric Thomas, PhD

RODALE.
NEW YORK

All rights reserved.
Published in the United States by Rodale Books, an imprint of
Random House, a division of Penguin Random House LLC, New York.
RodaleBooks.com
RandomHouseBooks.com

RODALE and the Plant colophon are registered trademarks
of Penguin Random House LLC.

Library of Congress Cataloging-in-Publication Data is available upon request.

ISBN 978-0-593-23498-3
Ebook ISBN 978-0-593-23499-0

Printed in the United States of America

Book design by Andrea Lau
Jacket design by Pete Garceau

10 9 8 7 6 5 4 3 2 1

First Edition

I want to dedicate this book to my wife Dede and all the people like Dede who got hit hard by life, but who, instead of giving up, decided to face it head-on and overcome the obstacle.

CONTENTS

CONTENTS

If you can't fly then run,
if you can't run then walk,
if you can't walk then crawl,
but whatever you do,
you have to keep moving forward.

—MARTIN LUTHER KING JR.

FOREWORD

The first time I heard ET's voice, I became an instant fan. There's something about it—the passion, the drive, the dog. Every time it gets me. For years, E has been sending me messages before games or when he knows I'm going through something, and when his voice comes on, it always has an impact. E's work is timeless. You can go on YouTube and watch one of his speeches and the only way you can tell when it's from is by looking at the time stamp. When he talks, it's like a sermon. If you've ever been to church and you hear the pastor speaking, and you think, *Man, he must be talking to me*, that's how it is to hear ET speak. It always feels like he's talking directly to you.

E's work and legacy make me think of my grandfather, who opened the first Black-owned service station in North Carolina. It makes me think of my father, who coached me and my brother through sports and through life. It makes me think of my own kids, who I want to be proud of me and have the experience of success I've had in life. E talks about having a why. For me, my why used to be that I hated losing more than

I liked winning. Over the years it's changed. When I first came into the NBA, I felt like I had to prove myself—to the league, to my family, to everyone I grew up with. Now I get a chance to show my kids what hard work looks like. I get to show them what preparation looks like. I get to show them what commitment looks like. I think E does that for all of us. Shows us what hard work and commitment look like.

In my own career, I'm drawn to people like me. I'm in my seventeenth season and I still feel the way I felt in the beginning—you will not outwork me. I'm drawn to people with the same work ethic. Sometimes you can just look in a person's eyes and tell they're a dog. People like that can be on my team any day. You can look at ET and see his grind. You can see his passion and his commitment. He's flown across the country to come see me play. He's come to speak at my youth leadership camps all over the United States. He shows up 100 percent every time without asking for anything in return. And it's not just for me. It's for everybody. I've seen him give his phone number out to kids because he could tell they needed someone to talk to. He does it because it's his calling. It's his calling to coach us all in whatever way we need it. It's his calling to be on *our* team.

We have this in common—E is on your team, too.

> —*Chris Paul*
> *NBA All-Star,*
> *philanthropist,*
> *and entrepreneur*

You Are The Only One Who Can Change Your Life

If you're holding this book in your hands right now, this book is for you. I wrote it for you. You might think that sounds crazy, that thousands of people are holding this very same book in their hands, reading this very same line, but it's true. I'm speaking directly to you.

You Owe You is a manual to help you understand your power and your purpose. It's a guide, illustrated with many of my own struggles and triumphs, to lead you toward your why and bring you closer to fulfilling your potential. This book is for you, wherever you are on your journey toward greatness. It's a book with an urgent message to stop waiting for the stars to align, to stop waiting for inspiration to strike, to wake up and take hold of your own life. Today. You owe it to yourself to become fully, authentically you. To live your life in the way that only you can live it.

I wish that I'd had this kind of blueprint to put me on a path toward greatness. I spent so many years lost. I spent so much time without intention. I spent much too long not pursuing my purpose. Maybe, if I had had this book, I would have seen my gifts and my power for what they were much earlier in my life. Maybe if I'd had this book, I wouldn't have spent so many years feeling like a victim, feeling alone, consumed with what other people thought about me.

Through much stumbling and many missteps, I finally found my path toward purpose. And today I am blessed to speak to an audience that is as large as it is diverse. I am now an internationally known speaker and motivational coach. And I am fortunate to work with rich people. Poor people. Black people. White people. Middle-aged people. Octogenarians even. I speak to famous people and people who stop me on the street because they know my name.

But the first people to start following me were kids. This is because, way back in the day, I started working with kids first. In college, I spoke to my peers at Oakwood in Huntsville, Alabama. And then I started helping high school dropouts get their GEDs, just as somebody helped me years before. I worked in elementary schools and middle schools. I visited juvenile detention centers and foster homes. I taught English and drama and speech in Huntsville, and I tutored kids who struggled in school, just as I did. Through all this work, I became known as ET, the hip-hop preacher.

When YouTube started, kids were the first ones to pick up on my videos. And, eventually, some of those kids got successful. They became college athletes or professional athletes. They became entrepreneurs and educators. They became comedians and actors and musicians. Those kids grew up and they took me with them. Kids are the ones I owe this book to. Especially kids who grew up without fathers, kids who struggled with learning disabilities or trauma, kids who were troublemakers like me.

When I go to schools, when I go to prisons, when I go to NBA locker rooms and NFL training camps, when I go to Australia or LA or Detroit or London or Alabama or France, the reaction is the same: They all hear me, and they all know I'm speaking to them. Telling them that *this* is the moment. This is life or death. This is the time you get up and change your life. It's not about money, it's not about fame, it's not about the degree or the touchdown or the check at the end of the grind. It's about getting up every day, understanding your power, walking in your purpose, knowing what you want, and spending every minute of the rest of your life going after it.

This book is informed by so many books I've read before it: Dennis Kimbro's *Think and Grow Rich: A Black Choice*, Dr. Na'im Akbar's *Visions for Black Men*, M. Scott Peck's *The Road Less Traveled*—and my own experiences self-publishing books like *The Secret to Success* and *The Grind*—but I hope that my book is unique in its delivery. So much of the work I've read before is difficult, academic, and complex. My message is deep, but it's also simple. I want you to be able to read this book and understand its message if you are twelve years old or forty years old. I want you to be able to read this book no matter where you're from or how far you've gone in school. I want my message to be clear to everyone.

My message is that you are the only one who can change your life. You are the only person who determines your value. You are the only person who can truly choose your purpose and find your path to greatness. You are the only person who can identify your difference and use it to your advantage. You are the only person who can help yourself.

I have been where you are. I am speaking to everyone who feels that they are living on the outside. Everybody who feels that the world wasn't built for them. There is common experience in struggling to understand a language that you don't know exists. There is common experience in feeling life or death urgency for whatever it is you have going on—raising your kids, making the rent, caring for your sick spouse, playing the most important game of your life, taking a test that makes the difference between staying in school and getting kicked out. We are human. We all feel these things if we allow ourselves to. So, when I'm speaking to my people, I'm speaking to you.

Because my work is inextricable from me, my work has always been about what it means to be a Black man in this country, trying to attain the American dream. But this does not mean playing the victim to any factor of my circumstances—race, gender, age, or socioeconomic status. This means writing your own narrative and claiming your place in the world, no matter what the world's perception of you is. I have acted like a victim before. I thought the world was happening to me. I became homeless. I turned my back on my family and refused to take responsibility for my choices. I ate out of trash cans. I slept in abandoned buildings. I made decisions that put me in those positions, and I denied my part in all of it. I took on a victim mentality, and eventually I saw my way out of it to become a victor.

In reality, there are many secrets to success. One of them is wanting to succeed as bad as you want to breathe. But this is only the beginning. Being successful is also about knowing that the only person in the way of your success is you. It's about seeing your power, and then finding your purpose and walking in it. It's about getting to know yourself, and seeing so clearly who you are that you can respond to the world around you and discover opportunity in return. It's about finding your why—your reason for getting up in the morning and grinding. It's about knowing when you have to give up something good for something great. It's about stretching toward your potential. It's about seeing that, at some point, you owe it to yourself to be great.

Even if you just became aware of me, I've been around a long time. I've been grinding at this speaking thing for over thirty years. But I'm also a pastor, an educator, and a counselor. I coach professional athletes one-on-one. I work with members of my community through marriage and family counseling. I pray with thousands of people every week, all around the world. I teach at universities and in prisons. I work with CEOs of Fortune 500 companies on team-building and personal growth. Every part of my work comes from having done my own personal work, struggling through my own issues, getting educated, and grinding toward excellence. I've been figuring out who I am and what my purpose is my whole life. Every day, I am reaching toward my potential, waking up for my why, giving up good things to get to great things. Truly, it has been a long road. I'm here to tell you that it was worth it. The journey is everything. The whole point is the journey. I didn't get here by wishing for it. I got here because I took myself on a trip. And I'm still on it. And, now, so are you.

CHAPTER

It's You versus You

WHEN YOU TAKE OWNERSHIP, YOU BECOME THE CEO OF YOUR LIFE.

Today, I walk into places of unimaginable privilege, from NBA locker rooms to the boardrooms of Fortune 500 companies. But my younger self would never have dared to imagine that the boy playing on the block in Detroit could have such a life.

When I was growing up, there weren't many expectations for me. I was born in Chicago, and raised in Detroit in the 1970s. Back then, if you were blue collar in Detroit, your destiny was already dictated: You graduated from high school; got a job at Ford, General Motors, or Chrysler; started a family; worked on the assembly line for the next forty years; retired; and collected Social Security. That was how my life was supposed to go. And that wouldn't have been a bad way to do it. That's how my parents did it. That's how plenty of people did it back in the day, and that was a sweet life.

Here's what you have to remember: There weren't many expectations because it was just good that we were living. My great-grandparents were sharecroppers. Their parents had been enslaved. That my parents owned a house and had cars, that my mom had a garden to tend and a job at Ford Motor Company to go to every day, was beyond any expectation her ancestors had ever dreamed of. When survival is the goal, how can you even think about what your higher purpose might be?

Just so you can understand how I grew up, I have to tell you about how my mom, Vernessa Craig, grew up. If you ask Vernessa what was expected of her, she'll tell you: nothing. She'll tell you about how she made it in the 1960s in Chicago at the height of segregation. She'll tell you that as one of fourteen children in an eight-hundred-square-foot apartment on the South Side, there were no expectations of her because there wasn't a lot of hope for her to begin with.

Her grandparents were born in the Jim Crow era, a time when African Americans were bound by the color of their skin, and weren't allowed to share space with white people. Train cars, water fountains, restrooms, hotels—my family was barred from the dignity of communing in public places with white people. My mother's father was from outside of Selma, Alabama. Her mother came from Sardas, Alabama. These places were impoverished, rural, and still operating on a system that was basically slavery in all but name. Their families scraped together a living based on indentured servitude, giving up a share of their crops to the landowner in order to survive. But, like six million other African Americans over the course of about sixty-five years, they eventually picked up their lives and struck out for some better future up North.

Both of my grandparents, Jessie McWilliams and Mary Craig, and their parents landed in Detroit around 1940. They'd all traveled by train as children up from Alabama, and settled in a neighborhood called Black Bottom, which was famous for its tight-knit Black community. There, they all worked together, fed each other, and looked out for one another.

One of eight children, Jessie McWilliams—the son of Eva and Aaron McWilliams—came over from Ireland with his parents during the potato famine. Jessie was biracial and lighter skinned, passing as Cuban or Italian, so he could move through the world more freely than a Black man might.

My maternal great-grandmother, Kate Gardner, died giving birth to my grandmother, Mary Kate Craig. My mother talks about what a large hole it left in Mary's spirit, and how she was withdrawn and distant most of her life. She never spoke about her past. The only child of her parents, Mary was raised by a stepmother who was essentially her wet nurse and had ten other children with Mary's father, Fred. She always felt alienated; she couldn't connect to the rest of the family. I can remember it as a kid, feeling that my grandmother was serious and businesslike—a true provider, focused on getting her family what they needed to make it to the next day. Of course, as a child I didn't understand why my grandmother seemed distant. But thinking about how these women grew up and raised children and raised themselves without the help of anyone else, I can see now how it might have kept them from expressing their full range of emotions.

My grandparents Mary Craig and Jessie McWilliams met in Detroit, had three children, and never got married. Eventually, Jessie took off. Mary met Mr. Braxton, my mom's stepfather, and they moved to Chicago and had eleven more children. My mother grew up thinking that her father was dead, until one day he showed up when she was ten or eleven years old, and she didn't know him from Adam. She remembers how her father looked white and the woman he came with, her stepmother, Bernice, was white. It took her a long time to accept who he was, but eventually they got close and Bernice fought to normalize their relationship. Her stepfather's family favored his kids, who were darker, more than her and her two sisters, but despite the complicated bloodlines, the kids grew up treating each other as full siblings and disregarding the politics of the shades of their Blackness.

My point in explaining the tangled dynamics of my family tree is to show you how my own personal history was built on a foundation of instability. There was no certainty for my family in society, just as there was

11

no certainty for them in their private lives. There was constant upheaval, constant worry about having the very basics of survival. There was a pattern of men disappearing while the women were left to fend for themselves and their children. It created a dynamic of dysfunction and a cycle of unpredictability. How can you think about creating a life of fulfillment when you're living in abject poverty?

Vernessa Craig got pregnant at seventeen and gave birth to me at eighteen. She was top ten in her class at Dunbar High School, a vocational-technical school, where you were accepted based on exceptional test scores. But they kicked girls out of high school for being pregnant back then. Luckily, one of her counselors let her in on a secret that the school didn't like to share with pregnant girls: You could still graduate if you took and passed your tests. So she did. She tried to make it work with my biological father, a boy named Gerald Munday she met at Dunbar. She remembers him as different from the rest of the young men in her neighborhood. He wasn't a gangbanger and he wasn't a troublemaker. But, ultimately, he wasn't interested in helping her raise me, Eric Munday.

When Mom met Jesse Thomas, a 6-foot-8 man who had played basketball at Texas Southern, they started off as friends. It was 1972. She was twenty years old with a two-year-old son. Jesse thought he was gonna be with a tall woman, a volleyball player type. A housewife type. Mom is 5-foot-2, and she definitely isn't a housewife. But eventually they started talking, and he understood her and was drawn to her will and her intelligence. He said he wanted children, which meant I wasn't a deal breaker. In fact, he wanted to adopt me. They were married, Mom became Vernessa Thomas, and after Jesse convinced her to move to Detroit— a place where, if they worked hard, they could own a house, have a yard, find good jobs—Jesse petitioned the court for adoption. In 1974, I became Eric Thomas, Jesse's son. They never told me I had a different biological father. That's just the way it was. And that's what I grew up thinking.

In Detroit, they rented for a while, but eventually settled at 8 Mile and Braile in a three-bedroom brick house on a corner lot. Mom had never imagined that she could own a house or have that kind of life, but she'd worked hard to get it and she loved it. Back then, there were still racial boundaries. The city, like most American cities, was segregated. You weren't supposed to go two blocks north of 8 Mile. We would venture as far as 7 Mile on occasion, but we didn't go to 6 Mile or 9 Mile. There was an unspoken one-mile-radius rule.

While I was growing up, Detroit was beautiful. It was vibrant. We had pride for the city that ran deep. The middle American ideal *was* Detroit. The whole world was listening to our music and driving our cars. In those days, Coleman Young was the city's first Black mayor and Motown was at the top of the charts—the Temptations, the Supremes, the Isley Brothers, the Clark Sisters. We'd hear that Diana Ross was in town, or that Michael Jackson was rolling in, and my friends and I would hang around the corner, looking into the distance, pretending we might catch a glimpse of a limo on its way to Berry Gordy's blue stucco studio. My grandma lived around there, and just being in proximity of it made you feel a buzz. Detroit was also all about civil rights in those days. You'd hear about Rosa Parks being downtown speaking, and sometimes the adults would talk about the time that Martin Luther King Jr. gave his Walk to Freedom speech. The memory of Malcolm X, who'd spent time in Lansing and had been assassinated only a decade before, was still very much alive.

As I still do today, I used to wake up before everybody else. Crack of dawn I'd be out on the block waiting for my boys to get up, waiting for the old-timers to roll out of bed. All summer long, we would be gone all day, riding around, or playing football in the street. I thought I was going to be the next Carl Lewis, running the 100-meter dash in the Olympics. Or, if not that, then play in the NFL.

Almost every weekend, my mom would take my sisters and me back to Chicago to visit with family. Her siblings were all still there, and they were close. Summers in Chicago were lit. At night, people would bring their sound systems out to the corner, and everybody would be up in the joint, techno music blasting, dancing in the street. Chicago was a little rougher than Detroit, but my oldest cousin Randy was cool with everyone, so we knew we were safe. We'd go out to the docks to fish, to Dominic's for candy, steal boxes of cereal from the trains delivering groceries, watch the girls jump double Dutch. Life was comfortable, and I didn't know any different.

But around the time I got to be eleven or twelve, I was starting to question some things. I'd been hearing my neighbors talk. I listened to my aunts saying things. Some of the kids on the block used to tease me, telling me my daddy wasn't my daddy. Whenever we got competitive with one another, playing cards or basketball, we'd shoot the dozens and make "your mama" jokes. The comeback to me was always "That ain't your real daddy." Eventually, you start to question if there's a grain of truth in these things.

So one day after school, I went through the house. I went through shelves and boxes and closets until I found what I was looking for. There it was in my mom's bedroom in a top drawer: my birth certificate. The name under the "father" box was not Jesse Thomas. I was crushed, but I knew it was true. It was a truth I'd been avoiding because I didn't want to know. At the same time, I was also in disbelief. All I could think of was that I had been lied to. My whole family had been lying to me. The most devastating thing, though, was that my mom, the single most important person to me—the person who made me—had been lying to me all along.

I needed to hear it from her. So I called her at work. When I ask my mom about that day, she says that my voice sounded different when she picked up the phone. She says she knew something was wrong immediately. I told her I had to ask her a question. I told her that I would believe whatever she told me. So I asked her, point blank: Is my father who I think he is? And she told me what I already knew.

Looking back, it was pretty obvious. I grew up with three grandmas. My dad was 6-foot-8 and I was always the smallest kid in the neighborhood. He's darker than I am, and we look nothing alike. There were whisperings and innuendos. But when you're that age, you believe what you're told until you can't anymore.

Truth can make or break people. That day, something inside of me broke. Nothing was the same after that. A piece of knowledge fell into place and it choked out everything that felt good and right in the world. That feeling has stayed with me and become embedded in the fabric of who I am. Even today, I have to fight hard not to let it destroy me. What I felt was that I'd been deceived in the most fundamental way—that everyone had turned against me—and instead of facing it and working through it, I pushed away everyone who could help me and turned inward. This is where things started to go wrong for me.

When I found out that the father who raised me wasn't my biological father, I felt like something had been taken away from me, and I became aware of a part of myself that had always been missing. All of a sudden, it was like life was happening to me and I couldn't control or stop anything. I was in crisis and I was drowning in it.

On the road to success, you cannot afford to make excuses.

My way of dealing was by getting angry. I am an emotional creature, so instead of looking around collecting the empirical evidence, when things get hard, I just get inside of my feelings. I didn't want anything to do with my father. I saw him as an adversary. I think I must have internalized the fact that I had never made an emotional connection with him and I began to see him more and more as my mother's husband instead of my dad. I also began to see him as the disciplinarian and I resented him for it. In some way, I think I wanted my mother to choose between me and my father. And when all was said and done, despite the evidence, despite the fact that this man had stepped in and raised me as his own, despite the fact that my mother had found a stable provider to create a family with, I chose to believe that she had picked him over me.

I went to school counselors. I went to therapists. Family members talked to me. Neighbors talked to me. My mom tried everything she could to reconcile it, but none of it worked because I didn't want it to work. I felt like I was in a bad movie, sitting down, making small talk with shrinks who were total strangers. They'd hit the clock, and I was expected to talk about something so intimate and deep I didn't have the words for it. I felt like a rat in a laboratory. I didn't understand why I was the one who had to go to a counselor when it was my mom and dad who'd lied to me. I was so angry that I stopped listening to them altogether. I started acting out, skipping school, and sleeping at friends' houses. At the age of twelve, I started leaving the crib, and by sixteen I'd left home altogether.

The argument that brought me to a breaking point took place on a weekend in March of my junior year in high school. My parents had gone to Chicago with my two little sisters, Jeneco, who was eleven, and Malori, who was two. While they were away, I threw a party at the house with my boys and ate up all the food, including some steaks Mom had bought for my dad. We cooked on the grill, my boys drank beers, and we all sat around pretending to act like men. When my parents got home, my father went looking for the steaks, and then he saw that the grill was dirty and the trash cans were full. When Mom told me to sit down, I refused. My dad told me to stop disrespecting my mom, and I started walking away. Before I could get past him, he grabbed my arm and I lost it. Up until that point, I hadn't said a word. I'd spent so long bottling up my feelings, suffering in silence, that I was like a train moving full steam ahead. I'd never cussed my mom out before. Never. And then I couldn't help myself. I let loose, and said some ugly things. In my mind, my parents were being hypocrites—they were all about respect and integrity, but then when it came down to the vital details of my life, I felt like they had disrespected me and kept me in the dark. My anger and bitterness had come to a head and couldn't be contained anymore. I stormed out of the house. It was a Sunday afternoon. Everybody in the neighborhood was out and everybody saw.

That day, something else in me broke. I felt as if I had come to the end of a very long road, and the only thing left to do was veer off it and go my own way. I didn't want anyone telling me what to do anymore, especially someone I felt didn't have the authority to be telling me what to do. I walked out of the house for good. I left with the clothes on my back and nothing else. That first night I slept in the backyard between the bushes and the wall of the house. March in Detroit is wet and slushy and gray. By the morning my bones were stiff with cold, but I felt like anything was better than going back. When the bus came, I had never been more excited to go to school. I wore the same clothes for two or three days, and slept in the backyard a couple more times. Eventually, I started wandering farther and farther away from home.

Around the time I left home, Detroit was getting rougher. It was 1986, and the YBI gang, the Young Boys Incorporated, was coming up, selling drugs in the city. The white people were moving farther and farther from downtown. Some nights I could sleep at a friend's, but other nights I was sleeping in empty buildings, freezing and hungry. I'd hear rodents scurrying by my head and gunfire outside. I couldn't stay in one place more than two or three days at a time because people might catch on to my habits, take everything from me, or worse. I was so hungry that

I started picking through dumpsters at grocery stores where they'd throw things out past their expiration date or looking through the trash near fast food joints where they'd toss leftovers after a shift.

You can change environments, but until you change yourself, nothing will ever change.

When I walked out of my home, I had nothing. I was so ignorant, I didn't think about what I'd do for shelter or food or warmth. I didn't have any ID, I didn't have any cash, I didn't have any clean clothes. And there weren't cell phones back then. If I wanted to talk to someone, I had to get on the pay phone or go find them. But the reality of my situation didn't actually hit me until about a week after I'd left. I remember I was walking along 12 Mile near Evergreen when rain started pouring down. All I had was a Starter jacket and a baseball cap. I ducked into a liquor store, bought some red Faygo and barbecue chips, and tried to look busy for a while, but when you're a Black teenager wandering around an

Arabic-owned liquor store in Detroit, you can only go up and down the aisles so many times before someone gets suspicious.

Soon after that night, I called my mom and while she didn't agree with my decision to leave, she continued to love and support me when I'd let her. And she even helped me get my license and blessed me with a car so I had a way to get around. Sometimes I'd sleep in it when I couldn't stay with a friend or when it was too cold to be in an open building. But sleeping on the streets wasn't sustainable and it wasn't safe, so I took a graveyard shift at McDonald's, working from 5 p.m. to 5 a.m. so that I had a place to be at night. It was a twenty-four-hour McDonald's on Finkle and Wyoming. I started the dinner shift and I kept going into the breakfast shift. And all the while I was still going to school, trying to hide the fact that I was homeless. After my graveyard shift at McD's, I'd have another few hours before I had to be at school, so I'd stop by a friend's house whose mom had to leave for work at 6 a.m. and catch some sleep.

I guess I didn't think of myself as being homeless at the time. I just wasn't living at home. I spent so much time alone in the dark that I started to get dark, too. I felt like I had no control over anything. I got resentful. I was still so angry. I blamed my mom and the father who was raising me for everything that was going wrong in my life. There were times I thought about doing bad things to myself. I never had a plan to do anything specific; I just let myself slip into a depression that was like a fog I couldn't see through. When I tell you all of this today, I can assure you that this state was against my nature. I'm not prone to depression or mental illness—that's a challenge that would have complicated things much further, I know. I'm a naturally optimistic, upbeat, social person. My natural state is effusive and energetic. I thrive when I'm with people.

But when I left home, I chose to be a victim of my circumstances. I chose to start hurting myself.

When you're young, your parents tell you what to do. They give you what you need to survive. They decide what you wear, what you eat, show you how to walk and talk. They pick you up from school and they pay the bills for the house you live in. Even if they're not teaching you, they're teaching you by example. When you're a kid, you're blissfully unaware that you will one day be responsible for yourself. And then one day, it's all you. From then on, nobody owes you anything anymore.

Being homeless was something I did. I chose it. I made myself into a victim because I thought the world had mistreated me. I thought that my mom was at fault. I thought she chose her husband over me. I couldn't see then that what she had done was to find a strong man who provided for her and her family, a man who stepped up to the plate to raise me as his own. In my version of the story, I had been wronged. I was a victim. But, in reality, I was working against myself.

I dropped out of high school. Eventually, I got my GED and went to college, but even after that, even after I met my future wife Dede and we got married, I still played the victim. I played video games and skipped tests. I didn't turn in papers or study. And you know what? Just like I got kicked out of high school, I got kicked out of college, too. I kept assuming that somebody else was responsible for me. I kept thinking that somebody else was gonna come in and take over.

You Can Choose to Be a Victim or a Victor

Victimhood is a mind-set. It's an attitude you hold that pushes you to make certain decisions or act a certain way. Victimhood is when the world happens to you. It's when you depend on the world to dictate your life. Victimhood is when you wait for the world to provide you with the tools to move forward. It's when you cede control to someone or something. Here's the thing: When you let the world have the power, you're playing Russian roulette with your life. You don't know where you're going to land because you are not steering the car. But when you begin to take control, you'll find that you have the power to change your outlook and become a victor in your journey.

The reality is this: When crisis hit, I chose to be a victim. And in choosing to be a victim, I hurt myself. I held on to my hurt and I let it get inside me and take over. I was hell-bent on believing that someone else messed up my life, but nobody kicked me out of the house. Nobody told me to leave. And nobody was more hurt by my decision than I was. I *chose* to live in abandoned buildings. I *chose* to eat out of trash cans. I *chose* to take this thing further than it ever needed to go.

There are going to be plenty of times in your life when things go sideways. There are going to be times when you feel hurt. And you're allowed to be hurt. You can be upset and angry. But feelings are not facts. They are feelings. Facts are how you can move through your feelings. What I wish I could have told the sixteen-year-old Eric is this: You can be angry, but be angry in your house. Be in angry in your bedroom. You can be upset, but be upset with air conditioning and a roof over your head. You can be sad, but be sad with meals on the table and clean clothes on your back. You don't need to sabotage your whole life to have your feelings. You can have your feelings, but you don't need to be a victim.

Here's the cool thing: When you shed the victim mentality and take ownership, when you take responsibility, when you take control, you're

Meaningful success begins when we take ownership and responsibility for our part in the shortcomings of our life.

the boss. You are the CEO of your life. There is no part of your life that will be unsuccessful if you take ownership. The only person you are working against is yourself. It's you versus you. Once you realize that you're the only person standing in the way of your own progress, you can change the pattern.

When I think about somebody who defies victimhood, I think about Vernessa Craig. Despite not having expectations placed upon her, despite growing up on welfare, despite having fewer resources than I ever had, my mom never acted like a victim of her circumstances. She had that dog. And she knew nobody was going to give her anything.

After being assaulted at the age of nine or ten, she became mute for a while as a result of the trauma. She was ridiculed by her peers, and spent all her time reading. In all the books she read, she saw that there was a way to happiness—that there was a world on the other side of hers and she was determined to find her place in it. When she got pregnant with me, she could have been thrown off her path, but it made her even more resolved to get off welfare and provide for me as an independent person. Back in those days, welfare was available to women who had kids, but didn't have a man in the house. She checked both boxes. But she worked hard. Vernessa got her first job at the age of fourteen and eventually worked up to a position with the government at the Argonne National Lab, just outside of Chicago.

In 1973, Mom went down to the welfare office and told her caseworker that she was getting off welfare, but before she did, she needed a voucher so she could buy a washing machine and a bedroom set. He looked at her like she had some nerve asking for something so fancy, but he respected her for it and agreed. In those days, Black women were taught to be submissive, but she never was. Vernessa was always assertive, and always asked for what she wanted. Feeling as if she'd won a battle, she went over to the Polk Brothers furniture store on Cicero Street. That was on the wrong side of Halstead, but the store had nicer furniture than she could find in her neighborhood. After she bought the bedroom set, she started walking back to the bus stop. That side of town was a scary place for Black folks. There were places in Chicago where the white people would stare you down and make you feel unwanted, but on Cicero, they would say all kinds of things, and maybe start a fight. Some men started heckling my mom, calling her the N-word, trailing her and making her feel nervous. Thankfully, a bus pulled up and she got in as quickly as she could. She remembers the Black driver getting angry at her, making her promise she would never go back to Cicero again. She says he might have saved her from something terrible, but she also vowed that she wasn't going to live that way for the rest of her life.

When I think about this moment, imagining my mom walking around in a part of Chicago where she had no business being, getting herself a bedroom set that she couldn't afford, I can see it clear as day. Moms has always been that way. Despite the world she grew up in, despite the fact that the laws were against her, that the system was against her, that the powers that be looked at her as lesser than, she never acted like a victim of her circumstances.

When I think about how someone else I love moves through crisis productively, I think of my friend, the speaker Inky Johnson. Inky grew up in Kirkwood, Georgia, in a tiny house with fourteen people. Inky knew from day one that he was going to be a football star. The boy is 5-foot-9 and 180 pounds on a good day. But he worked hard. As a kid, he'd be running drills until the streetlights went off, and, even then, he'd keep going in the glow of his mom's car headlights. Eventually, he made it to the University of Tennessee as a starting cornerback. Inky was living his dream. Everybody knew his name and there was talk of a career in the NFL. Inky thought he might be able to buy a house for his mom, get his family set up with some savings. But in his sophomore year, in a game against Air Force, Inky tackled somebody so hard he had to be carried off the field. He almost died of internal bleeding. After hours of surgery and reconstructive work to repair blood vessel damage, Inky lost all use of his right arm. Everything he'd been working for up to that point was gone.

But here's the difference between the younger me and Inky Johnson. Inky did not treat himself like a victim. He didn't start walking around like something had been done to him, even though he might have been entitled to. He got up and went back to school. He went on to get a master's in sports psychology and then became a motivational speaker like myself. Inky, to me, is the epitome of the person who understands the battle of "you versus you." His body would no longer allow him to do the things he had dreamed of doing. His body turned against him in a way that could have left him hopeless, depressed, and without a career. But Inky saw this challenge, and he stepped up to it. He cast off the victim mentality and challenged himself to do something more. Inky overcame himself.

Look in the mirror, that's your competition.

How do you do this in your own life? How do you cast off the character of victim? How do you get out of your own way so you can move forward toward your purpose?

Number one: You have to take ownership of yourself. Your choices are your own and nobody else's. The same way you hold other people accountable for being late, or not paying you on time, or cutting you off at a stoplight, you have to hold yourself accountable. No matter where you are in life, you have the power to take ownership of it. So many of us start from behind. So many of us didn't even start at GO. My grandmother didn't have the opportunities my mom had. My mom didn't have the opportunities I have. Today, they sit back and are stunned at what they contributed to. They can't believe I am where I am. Or that my kids are where they are. But it's because they took ownership of their lives. It's because I took ownership of my life. I stopped playing victim and I took control.

When I became homeless, I had to deal with the fact that I had no purpose, no plan, no motivation, and no standards. At some point, I had pushed so many people away that I had to see that I was the only one responsible for putting myself in dangerous situations, for stealing food, for being cold and hungry. Nobody kicked me out of my house. Nobody told me I couldn't sleep in my own bed. Yes, my mother and my family had decided to keep information from me about my biological father, but that was their choice, not mine. While on one hand I was liberated from other people's choices about my life, I had not yet made the connection that I was now the one making choices, and those choices were my very own.

Number two: You have to own your decisions. Yes, crises happen. Jobs are lost. Family members get sick. Money can be tight. But if you tell yourself that you are a victim, you will not be able to work through these challenges. The challenges will work you over and you will lose control. Nobody's gonna stop you from scrolling on your phone all day. Nobody's gonna stop you from sitting on the couch and bingeing four hours of television. Nobody's gonna wake you up at 5 a.m. to go take a run or study for that test or go look for a job. That's all you. The only person who is going to do it for you is you.

Number three: Set a standard. When you don't have a benchmark, you let yourself free-fall. A goal is an intangible desire, but a standard is solid ground. You want to get into shape? Set an exercise and diet standard, and meet that standard. You want to buy a house for your family? Set a savings standard, and, while you're at it, pick up a book and start getting literate about your finances. You want to finish your degree? Set a standard to always do your homework, to memorize the material, to make your grades. Nobody is going to set standards for you. Nobody is going to read the books or go to classes for you. Only you can set a standard and follow through.

It took me twelve years to get a four-year degree. Part of that was because I didn't set enough standards for myself. When I started college, I didn't look at my life and think about what standard would get me from point A to point B. At that moment, I was overjoyed to have a place to sleep every night. My standard was so low that I couldn't see that my education was suffering. Eventually, when I was secure in my life, when I could see that the only way I could get to the next level was to finish my degree and then go on to get my PhD, I set a standard, I met that standard, and then I surpassed it.

Number four: No excuses. Once you set a standard, there is no room for making excuses. If you said you're going to do something, then do it. The mind never thinks of something that it is not capable of accomplishing. If you say you're going to get up at 5 a.m. and you don't, don't make an excuse. Own up to it. And then tomorrow, set your alarm and get up at 5 a.m. If you say you're going to do your homework, do the homework. Ain't no excuse for not doing it.

I used to let myself get away with not giving 120. It's not that I was unmotivated, it's that I had poor time-management skills and I wasn't living up to my fullest potential. First, I didn't have standards and I didn't have structure. These are necessary tools to getting you to the next level for sure, and I'll go into much more detail about how to build and use these tools later in this book. But, second, I also let myself get away with being unproductive and making poor choices. I always found a way to excuse myself for not going to classes or not doing the homework. Even later, after I got into college, there were always seemingly worthwhile reasons to make excuses—I had to teach a GED class or speak some-where on campus—but this is a choice and a matter of priorities. I let myself make excuses for not getting to the next level.

Once you realize that you're the only person standing in the way of your success, you will start to see progress, I promise you. There is no-body else who can change your circumstances but you.

Now consider this: As soon as you realize that you're responsible for yourself, you can look around and see that there are people who will support you. There are people who can help you move toward the stan-dard you're trying to reach. There are resources that you can rely on to make progress. Once you're working *with* yourself instead of *against* yourself, you can see that the only thing standing in the way of the rest of your life is you.

The Work

1. What was the last challenge you faced in your life, big or small? What was your first instinct when this challenge came up? How did you handle the challenge? What were the results? When did you last feel helpless, as if you weren't in control?

2. Now go back through that challenge or situation where you felt out of control, and analyze how you could have approached it

differently. See if you were in your feelings. Analyze the facts. Play out how the results might have changed if you had stepped outside of that challenge and walked all the way around it.

Challenge: Do you foresee a challenge ahead? Do the same exercise, projecting how you will handle it in the future. Play out the possibilities of what it would look like if you took control. Pause to consider how you might change the results of the challenge, based on how you handle the challenge.

CHAPTER

2

You Are Never in It by Yourself

YOU ARE ONLY ALONE WHEN YOU TELL YOURSELF YOU ARE ALONE.

Growing up, I think I internalized some deep stuff about slavery, inheritance, and my past. When I was a kid watching *Roots* or learning about the enslavement of my people in school, it all still felt so close to home. Why did I have to go to school and get a job somebody told me I had to get? Why did I have to follow somebody else's rules that didn't have anything to do with how I wanted to live my life? I felt that other people were trying to own my time and my mind. When my father who raised me disciplined me, I felt that he was playing the slave master. When my mom kept information from me, it felt like she was trying to manipulate the facts of my life. So, to gain back some control, I felt that I had to shut them both out. I was in that victim boy's mentality. And when I got into a victim mentality, I shut everybody out and started telling myself I was alone.

This is what I know now: If you tell yourself that you are alone, then you are alone. Aloneness is part of the victim mentality. This is the mindset of someone to whom things are happening. When you act like a victim, you close yourself off to communication and relationships. You pit yourself against the world. You dig yourself into a dark hole where no one else can see you or touch you. You close yourself off to potential solutions. But, in reality, you are never in it by yourself. The perception that it's you against the world is a construct. The world does not conspire against you. You conspire against you. It's you versus you. Nobody can tell you that you're alone but you.

When I found out that I had a biological father, I closed off all

> # People either inspire you to greatness or pull you down in to the gutter. No one fails alone, and no one succeeds alone.

channels for communication and solutions. I shut out everybody who had anything to do with my family—my aunts, my grandmas, my family, my friends. I thought to myself, "I am alone," and thus I was alone. But it wasn't true. My mom didn't go anywhere. We've been together since the day I was born. My aunts and my grandmothers, my father who raised me—they were all still around. It was me who left.

To get away from my family, I started spending more time outside my neighborhood, especially with my boy, Bob. His parents were both heroin addicts and his father was shot eight times and killed when Bob was in high school. His mom was still dealing with her own recovery when Bob's grandfather stepped in. Gramps—or Elder King as he was called at church—took Bob and his brothers Bill, Marky, and Wayne into his three-bedroom house on 7 Mile, where Bob's step-grandmother, her two grandkids, and her daughter were all living already. Gramps had finished the basement with four bunk beds, a bathroom, and a living area, which is where we spent most of our time.

7 Mile was a whole different world from 8 Mile. Where my neighborhood was closer to Southfield, a quieter, suburban kind of place, 7 Mile was right next to inner-city Detroit. Where 8 Mile was mostly nuclear families doing the Midwestern family thing—house, yard, kids, cars in the driveway, jobs at Ford, Chrysler, or GM—7 Mile was more multigenerational families. Some people had jobs and some people didn't. Just a mile and a few blocks over from my sheltered world, it was a whole different social and economic landscape. Some streets were nice, but if you walked down the wrong block you had to watch yourself.

Bob and I went to high school at Henry Ford and played sports together. On the weekends, Bob went to church, so if I wanted to hang out with him, I went, too. Detroit Center was a little hole in the wall church on Puritan and Ward. If you looked in through the front door, you could see right out the back. The floors were covered in thin red burgundy carpet and filled with wooden pews covered in blood-red cushions. Detroit Center was a Seventh-Day Adventist church, a type of Presbyterian faith that keeps Saturday, the seventh day of the Jewish and Christian calendar, sacred. There were about forty-five people who attended regularly—seven or eight families and some older folks, too. I had no idea I needed it, but Detroit Center was a home I'd been seeking out. And I felt like I had a support system again.

For as long as I can remember, I've always felt spiritual. Even though I didn't grow up going to church, I still prayed. My mom sent me to a religious camp when I was eight years old, and I read all the classic Bible stories kids love—David and Goliath, Joseph and the Pharaoh, Samson and Delilah. Religion isn't necessarily my thing—I don't care for the country club aspect of it all—but I love scripture. I still think the idea that Jesus, as an outsider Jew who came to save everybody, is beautiful. Beyond that, I'm just a man of the spirit. I now lead prayer circles with my friends and for NFL players, attend Bible study groups, and I'm the pastor of my own church community. But, for me, it's about being together and praying together. It's all about relationships. If the Jehovah's Witnesses knock on the door, I'll sit down and study with them. If you show up to my church and want to sing hymns and say the Lord's Prayer, you're more than welcome to. When I came into Detroit Center, I felt the same way. I just liked being in church with other people.

The congregation was run by Pastor P. C. Willis. He was a military man and a black belt in karate. Pastor Willis was probably 6-foot-1 or 6-foot-2, and always in good shape. When men walk into the same room with one another, we don't necessarily give automatic respect to one another. Male respect is something that has to be earned. But Pastor Willis was a man's man. He could walk into a room and command the respect of everybody within a minute. And when he got up to speak, he spoke with conviction. He was always speaking like it was an emergency. Like it was life or death. There was always a call to action. Whatever he was talking about felt like it was at the center of the world, and we should all be paying attention to it. When I think about my own way of speaking, I see us as a part of the same lineage.

Pastor Willis's family was like the Black Partridge Family. Him, his wife, his four daughters and a son. They all sang at church. They all did readings. They prayed with each other. It was like everything I'd ever seen on television. When I was in that room, I felt like I could see how life was supposed to be.

It's weird. Being homeless was the worst time in my life—never knowing where I was going to sleep, being embarrassed that I hadn't showered or changed clothes in three or four days, being alone in my head. But it was also one of the best times, too. I was free from the boundaries and rules of home, cruising around with my boys, soaking up the sounds of Detroit—hip-hop was our language in the 1980s—driving to Canada on the weekends, hitting Belle Isle in the summer in souped-up Suzukis and Jeeps. But I also found a new home that I'd never known could exist. By the end of the summer of 1987, I was all-in at Detroit Center. I spent weeknights and weekends at the church, singing, volunteering for revivals, raising my hand to help with this or that. It was like finding the family that I didn't know I could have. We would eat together, pray together, go to barbecues at people's homes. There was a sense of togetherness that was new but also familiar.

This feeling of chosen family, along with the newfound freedom I'd always craved, was powerful. I was making my own decisions. I was playing by my own rules and nobody was interfering. Nobody was telling me I couldn't do this or that. Nobody was whipping me for acting up or breaking the rules. Even when I was sleeping on the streets, I felt like my own person, like I was finding a part of myself and the world beyond the life that had been imposed on me.

Of course, there were moments when things were dark. Times when I'd be sleeping in a cold, echoing building, wondering if anything would ever be okay again, questioning if I would ever feel connected to anyone again. But when I got to a church service, I felt embraced and seen and loved. One of my strengths is that I'm a naturally positive person. I've always seen the glass as half-full. And I've always been attracted to people.

Talking and connecting with people is what gives me energy. It's how I recharge. So even when I chose to leave my house and my family, I naturally gravitated toward another kind of family.

When I found the church, it was the first time in my life that I selected people for myself. Everyone I'd been surrounded with before was in my life by virtue of family ties and geography. The people I knew were the people in our neighborhood, my family in Detroit and Chicago, my friends at school. When I found the church, it was the first time I began to form ideas that had not been imposed upon me. At church, there was time to just be present, to be fully in every moment—whether it was singing or praying or listening to Pastor Willis's deep voice in the middle of an impassioned sermon. There was no worry about what was coming next. When I began to explore the world independently, to ask questions and see the people and landscape around me with new eyes, I also began to discover fulfillment in choosing people I wanted to be around. Here was a family who gave me responsibility and found a use for my natural gifts. Here was a place I could find connection and fellowship in activities that were spiritually and intellectually nurturing.

The way I grew up was all about grinding to exist. That's the blue-collar mentality. You work and work and work some more. Grinding, where I'm from, is all about brawn. Getting up early, staying up late, and putting in overtime meant success. In Detroit, personal success was always based on your ability to produce. To get up every day for forty-five years and grind until that pension came. I could look at the older people in my neighborhood, and see their hands worked over with arthritis. I could see the parts of life they were missing out on, doing night shifts, not seeing their kids growing up.

Grinding, in the way I grew up, was necessary. But it's only one dimension of work. If you're only grinding, you can get worn down. Like a pestle against a mortar, your mind and your body can become eroded if you don't find another way to work. Over the years, grinding served me for a while. It's the only way I knew how to do things. But at church, and later in school, I learned that grinding isn't just about physical force. It's mental, too. It's a kind of powering through work and life with total commitment. It's a way of thinking about yourself holistically—asking what your mind can do, what your heart can do, what your brain can do. It's about working smarter, not necessarily harder. Today, I still grind, but I do it differently—with a goal beyond just existing. I grind to be fulfilled and to get closer to my purpose.

Surround Yourself with Support

Detroit Center was so small that whether I told my fellow congregants or not, they knew I was homeless. How could they not? I was showing up unwashed. I wore the same clothes all the time. Nobody was dropping me off at home or coming around to visit with my mom and dad. And, of course, they began to look after me in the ways that only a family can. I got fed and clothed. I got invited into people's homes for dinners and prayer circles. In opening myself up to being cared for, I found care.

I also found the woman I was going to marry.

Dede and I were friends first. She was raised by a single mother who had that grind mentality, too, and we were cut from the same cloth in a lot of ways. Dede was a caregiver and she was serious. She got good grades and she knew what was up ahead of her. She worked hard. At first I didn't tell Dede what was going on with me. I sold her on the fact that I had a car and was "living" in Lathrup Village, the nice suburban place I'd left behind. But, eventually, I told her what my situation was, and I think it endeared me to her. I think she looked at me and saw a project. She would let me come over when her mom was at work, and get me something to eat or tell me I could take a shower when it was obvious I hadn't had one in a while. She was kind to me, and helped me see what I needed even when I didn't see it myself. I think I was attracted to Dede not only because she was kind and compassionate but because she knew herself. Dede always knew what she wanted and she went after it.

In Dede I found somebody who saw me. In Detroit Center, I found a community who saw me. Although I had blocked myself off from my relatives, I still kept a part of myself open for connection. But this isn't always easy for other people. I'm an extrovert. No matter what's going on with me, I thrive on human connection. I have confidence in the fact that when I open my mouth, I will have something to say, and I have worked with my gift long enough to know that what I say will connect with whoever is listening.

But what happens when you're an introvert and your natural state is to crawl back into your shell or to retreat from the world? In reality, introverts are often much better equipped to communicate than extroverts. Extroverts may have the confidence and the natural inclination to be outgoing, but the introvert has the ability to be five or six steps ahead intellectually. Most of the world's billionaires are introverts. If you're an introvert, or you're working with one, it's important to be aware of keeping yourself open to communication. Because the introvert's natural state is in retreat from other people, you have to actively remind yourself that human support and connection are necessary to thriving. Introverts love clarity and transparency. If you're an introvert, communicate what kind of support you need and how you'd like to receive it. Practice the conversation ahead of time. Play out the potential scenarios in your mind. If you're working with an introvert, communicate what you need and want from them and be clear about what you can do and will give to reciprocate support.

I surround myself with the kind of people who can help me turn my life around, people I can rub up against like iron and be sharpened.

For many of the athletes I work with, finding the right kind of support is a challenge. When you get to that level, your entire life is about proximity. Your teammates, your coaches, your doctors—they are all part of the team's ecosystem. You made some choices to get where you are, but you're also hemmed into a structure that is not entirely within your control. Even when you're the best athlete on planet Earth, victim mentality can take hold and isolate you.

Some of the athletes I work with harbor resentment against their parents. So many times, I hear about fathers who didn't show up to games, who weren't present for the wins and the losses. When I hear this, I ask athletes to consider where their fathers were when they were playing. Oftentimes, the answer is "My dad was at work." So I ask them who dropped them off at practice or who paid for their shoes and uniforms. I ask them how they think those things got paid for. Victim mentality makes you see what hasn't been done for you as opposed to what *has* been done for you. I always say that where your focus goes your energy flows. If you're focusing on who wasn't there in your life or what you didn't get from them, it doesn't allow you to see who was there or how they were showing up in other ways.

The victim in you makes you get into your feelings as opposed to your brain. Feelings are valid, but they are not evidence. I worked with the UFC fighter Maycee Barber on untangling her feelings about her father's opinions of her profession. Maycee felt her dad wasn't supportive of her career in the sport. He had reservations about her becoming a fighter and potentially putting herself in harm's way. Maycee had a difficult time separating the idea of her dad as someone who loved and supported her from the idea of his disapproval of her participation in the sport. Working with her, I helped her to separate her feelings from the evidence—her father wasn't withdrawing his support from her; he was expressing his concern for her well-being. I helped her to see that he was still there to support her through the challenges, but that she also had to allow him the freedom to feel what he feels. Separating feelings from facts can help us unpack the complexity of human relationships and get ourselves out of a place of victimhood.

When I coach athletes, I tell them to set aside their feelings for a moment, and to look at the evidence. Often, the evidence shows that they could never have gotten to where they are alone. They needed other people—their coaches, their parents, their aunts and uncles, their grandparents, their friends, their teammates. The evidence is always there: You are not alone. You have support.

Now, there's another challenge to this aspect of surrounding yourself with and accepting the people around you as a support system. When you get to any level of success—monetary or otherwise—not everybody who wants to be around you is there for genuine reasons. There are people who want to run with you because you're moving up in the world, because you're famous, because you've got money, because you can dunk and make touchdowns. When you get to that level, you have to continue making choices based on evidence. Who nurtures you? Who gives you more than you give them? Who is on your team because you are you and not because they see you as a stack of money or a number on a jersey? Seeing the people around you clearly is necessary to combat the victim mentality. When you tell yourself you're alone, it can be easy to slip into relationships that are false or that fulfill a surface desire for praise or company or pleasure. In constantly evaluating your own behaviors and patterns and seeking evidence over emotion, not only will you be able to see yourself better, but you'll also gain a clearer view of the people who surround you.

To find support, you have to be open to accepting support. When you close off communication, you close yourself off to the possibility of accepting help. A friend of mine, Charles, likes to tell a story about his son Jackson. From a young age, Jackson has always had an independent spirit. When he turned three, he started to wake up, go downstairs, and pour himself a bowl of cereal in the morning. But there was a milk problem. Here was a little kid, trying to lift a gallon of milk all by himself, and every time, he'd spill it everywhere. Charles wanted to help Jackson, but Jackson wouldn't let him. Finally, Charles showed him that he could put the milk in a smaller container especially for him, and he could still come downstairs and make his cereal on his own without spilling the milk all over the kitchen floor. If you're having difficulty accomplishing something alone, there is no shame in reaching out for help. Sometimes, to get to the next level, you need support. And to get support, you have to be willing to let down your guard and accept it.

There's one more important step to seeing and accepting that you are not alone in this world. Once you've realized your ability to connect and to choose the relationships that will support and nurture you, you have to understand and acknowledge the parts of yourself that want to choose victimhood over connection, the pieces of you that might continue to whisper that you are alone and you are unloved.

When I discovered that the father who raised me was not my biological father, something inside of me broke and would never be fully repaired again. There was a schism in my emotional development that caused me to turn inward and push away the people who had loved me and nurtured me all my life. Just because I've repaired my relationship with my mom and my father who raised me and my aunts and everyone else I thought had been deceiving me does not mean that the part of myself that broke will ever be fully healed.

The ET you know—the larger-than-life, happy-go-lucky guy who hugs and fist-bumps everybody when he walks into a room—he is not the only Eric Thomas who exists. Part of me can still see the world as a place that's as dark and cold as the run-down buildings I slept in when I was homeless. There is still an Eric Thomas who can feel hard and angry about being lied to. And when this Eric shows up, it can be jarring to the people who only know the other version of me.

I'll give you an example. I was on a work trip with my business partners CJ and Josh. Now CJ is my boy and my best friend. We've been together since the day we met at Michigan State in 2006. We talk every day, all day. We travel together. Our families are tight, and he knows just about every detail of my life. Aside from Dede, ain't nobody closer than C.

When we were on this trip, I started seeing CJ and Josh getting together—having breakfast or a drink—and I hadn't been told about these meetings. To me, it looked like they were meeting behind my back, as if I were purposefully being left out. The Eric inside me who felt that he had been deceived or conspired against by my mom started to whisper in my ear, telling me that CJ and Josh were doing something behind my back, manipulating me, or pushing me out. The Eric who was wounded back in the day, the unhealed part of me, started to come out and get suspicious.

But the difference between me and the sixteen-year-old ET is that I am aware of this defensive, colder part of myself. I can see this part of me who wants to act like the victim boy and I can tell him to stay in check. When I start to feel like a victim, I know I start to get in my feelings instead of looking at the evidence. To get out of my feelings, I go through the exercise of gathering facts. In this situation, I started asking myself if there was any reason I shouldn't trust CJ. What I know about CJ is this: He quit his job as a substitute teacher in his early twenties to come take a job with me that didn't guarantee any money. He and his wife Candis, who also works with us, traveled everywhere with me, and made sure that our business was solid. CJ didn't take a paycheck for a long time, in order to build my career. CJ gave up his own speaking career to focus on getting me to the top of the field. CJ negotiates my speaking rates and has gone to bat for me on my non-negotiables and triple-checks every single person who comes into my life to make sure they are genuine and well-meaning. CJ has always had my back.

Because I am aware of this ugly part of my personality, the part of me that is still broken and unhealed, I'm able to find my way through it when it begins to show up again. I'm able to look around myself to see that I'm not actually alone or helpless or out of control. I can be aware that the baggage I carry around from past relationships does not need to be transferred into my current relationships.

So instead of turning away from CJ, as I might have twenty years ago, I turned toward him and asked him why he and Josh and Jemal were meeting without me. The truth was that they were working on a business plan that would help grow and support our company as a whole and my financial longevity. They were working on building investments and passive income so I would never have to work again if I didn't want to. When I saw them meeting without me, the part of me that acts like a victim couldn't have imagined the possibility that they were trying to help me. That part of me could only see was that I was not included.

At the time, I was spending more time with my wife Dede, helping her with her recent diagnosis of multiple sclerosis. I couldn't speak or travel as much as I did when she was well. CJ recognized that to keep our company thriving, he needed to find an alternative path to stability that didn't depend on me traveling 24/7. Also, in the beginning stages of building our company, I did not perceive myself to be good at or interested in business. I considered myself an entirely relational person—a communicator and relationship-builder. I closed myself off to getting educated about the business side of things. This is why my relationship with CJ is vital. He has never been afraid to be a businessperson, and prides himself on being the pilot of our company. Because I'm aware of my weaknesses, I surround myself with people who are good at what I am not. When Josh and CJ were meeting without me, it wasn't because they were conspiring against me. It was because they were taking care of me and working to make sure that I could continue to nurture my superpower without having to worry about speaking into my old age. When I chose to communicate and evaluate the evidence of this situation, my full self was able to show up and see the support that was being offered to me. I could see that I wasn't alone.

A real friendship is not about what you can get, but what you can give. Real friendship is about making sacrifices and investing in people to help them improve their lives.

The other part of recognizing that you aren't alone is coming to the realization that you have a self. And once you are aware of your selfhood, you must articulate that full self to the people who show up to support you. CJ is also aware of the part of my personality that shows up like a victim because I've talked to him about it. I came to our relationship with all the information about my past and my shortcomings. The part of me that tends toward victimhood is so different from the other parts of my personality that when that victim boy shows up, it can be hard for people to see. It can make people feel that they don't know me, and people recoil when they feel they've been deceived. Think about it. If you show up all extroverted to work every day, bubbly and throwing up high fives, and then one day come in evasive and angry, your coworkers are going to be shocked and withdraw from you. The broken parts of you are just as important as the healthy parts. They all need to be seen and acknowledged for you to remain connected to the rest of the world—to feel that you're fully seen and supported.

I'll give you another example. When Dennis Rodman got traded to the Chicago Bulls in 1995, his full self was on display. He didn't hide his desire to party or shut down his flamboyance or change the way he looked to conform to the rest of the NBA. He came to Phil Jackson and Michael Jordan with all the information about his difficult past and itinerant childhood. And because he articulated and displayed his full personality, he was able to become his full self on the court—unselfish and totally supportive. When Rodman gave himself to the Bulls, Jackson and the team were able to give him reciprocal support to succeed. When he left to blow off steam in Vegas during the height of the '98 season, Jackson and Jordan and Scottie Pippen, to some extent, understood. If Dennis Rodman had pushed away the parts of himself that inform what we equate with the singular Dennis Rodman, we may not have had the magnificent alchemy of the Bulls' 1998 season.

Another aspect of bringing your full self to the table is understanding what your strengths and weaknesses are. If you can communicate these effectively, you can be supportive and find the support you need in turn.

Part of my strategy in coaching companies, teams, and individuals is to use the Flight Assessment, a self-assessment tool that my team created, based on the DISC Index. The DISC is based on emotional and behavioral theory that separates personalities into Decisive, Interactive, Stability, and Cautious types. It helps you understand how you work on teams and adapt to the environments around you. My team adapted this to our own system of self-assessment that determines your behavioral style to bring to light how you like to get things done. It's a helpful tool to become more self-aware. For me, the Flight Assessment helped me gain insight into how I could perform more effectively and in what roles I was at my best. There are four different behavioral styles: The Pilots are the big-picture thinkers who want immediate results and need to be in the driver's seat; the Flight Attendants are innovative, connect through emotion, and are motivated by being with others; the Grounds Crew are agreeable, sociable, nonthreatening, and prefer to support others; and the Air Traffic Controllers are factual, logical, motivated by solving complex problems, and thrive with structure.

Everybody has aspects of each of these behavioral approaches to their lives, but we are naturally stronger in one style than others. Our approaches shift depending on whether we are in our natural state or in an adaptive state and have to adjust to the people around us. The best teams and companies are built around people who have different natural and adaptive behavioral styles. When we become aware of the way we approach the world around us, we're able to give and receive support more effectively to achieve peak performance as a group and as individuals.

I am a Flight Attendant, which means I am super relational and social. I love meeting and talking to new people. I'm also impulsive and emotional. Because I'm aware of these aspects of my behavior, I can now sit back and see when I'm in my feelings and when I need to think through them with more intention and logic. In the case of CJ and Josh and Jemal meeting without me, where I felt I was being left out and kept in the dark, I could step back and see that I needed to spend some time in introspection, thinking through my feelings, setting them aside, and evaluating the facts.

On the other side of that situation is CJ, who is a Pilot. He's demanding and assertive. He likes to solve problems quickly and directly. Sometimes this manifests in making decisions without necessarily thinking through the risks or alternative possibilities. His strength is flying the plane, not necessarily communicating how to fly it. When he started working with Josh and Jemal on other businesses, he was doing it because it was a solution to the problem at hand. My wife was sick and I wasn't able to go on the road as much as I used to. CJ is twelve years younger than me, and he didn't want me to worry about working forever if I didn't want to or couldn't be available to. He wanted to make sure that he and his own family, as well as the rest of our team, were able to be secure in their lives if I wasn't able to be the face of our company.

Because we are aware of one another's behavioral styles, we're able to work more effectively together and to provide each other with the support we need to be working at our highest potential. I realized that I was being in my Flight Attendant mode and he saw that he was being in his

Pilot mode, and we could come back together to understand how to best be there for each other.

Take your own free Flight Assessment at ETYouOweYou.com

In 2021, before the NCAA championship, I worked with Baylor's men's basketball team to help the players and coaches see how they function in connection with one another. Each of the coaches and players took the Flight Assessment, and then I spent time with the coaching staff to help them see their players as individuals and understand how each of those individuals needed a different kind of support to reach their full potential. In Baylor's case it was a matter of simplification. No one player needed to be everything to everybody. The Flight Attendants needed to be out there talking and encouraging everyone and the Pilots needed to be making good decisions. The Air Traffic Controllers needed to be paying attention to the plays and the Grounds Crew needed to be rebounding and making assists. Guys who were good at putting up twenty points needed to realize that they had to work harder to put up thirty points. Guys who are good at assists needed to realize that 90 percent of assists had to land.

That year, Baylor went on to win the chip, and Coach Scott Drew credited me with helping him and his staff to see their players in a new way. With all the information, they found a new way to provide the team with tremendous support and the communication needed to get to the next level. When they felt that they were seen, each player became a lot less lonely. When given the support they needed, each player was able to reach their full potential in the most vital moments. When we become self-aware enough to articulate our strengths and weaknesses, and to see the strengths and weaknesses in other people, we suddenly have a new way of seeing the world and interacting with it.

When I chose to become homeless, I did not have the ability to see the support around me. I was not self-aware enough to know how to deal with my own strengths and weaknesses. I could not see support or seek support or support others because I was not open to the connections and solutions.

Now consider this: I didn't need to become homeless to discover my freedom. I didn't need to sleep in abandoned buildings to find a new kind of community that would take care of me. I didn't need to eat out of trash cans or live in the back of my car or steal groceries to have people bring me into their lives and support me. I had no business doing any of that. I had no business leaving home and turning away from the people who had always been there for me. The only thing I really needed to do to discover and take hold of my freedom was to understand that I was never alone in the first place. At some point, when I became actualized enough as an adult, I even opened myself up to a relationship with my biological father. Today, we talk regularly and, though our connection isn't perfect, I'm always thinking about how to work on it.

The Work

1. Are there moments where you feel alone or without support? When you do feel lonely, what triggers this feeling? Do you have a strategy for how to deal with these moments? Do you have a support system you can reach out to?

2. Are there moments when your feelings overwhelm you or cloud your judgment? Or, on the flip side, are there moments when you should be emotional, but are overly practical? Make a list of these situations and the things that trigger your reaction.

3. Ice Cube has that great line: "You better check yo self before you wreck yo self." Do you have a way of checking yourself? Do you have a way of assessing yourself? Are you aware of what triggers you to shut down communication? Are you aware of the wounded parts of yourself? Make a list of the parts of you that are hurt and how they show up in your everyday interactions.

Challenge: Recall the last time you felt that you were alone. Think about the way you reacted to feeling alone. Did you reach out to someone or remain in seclusion? Make a plan of action for when you start to feel that you're alone. Make a list of people you could reach out to for support. Write down the kind of support you would like to receive—a listening ear, someone who can offer solutions, a hug, someone who will ask questions or just sit with you.

CHAPTER

3

Discover Your Superpower

WHEN YOU FIND AND CHANNEL YOUR SUPERPOWER, YOU MOVE TOWARD YOUR PATH OF PURPOSE.

When I was really young, I was a true mama's boy, always wanting to be close, always up under my mom. Of course, because I was her only child at the time, we were super tight. But when I was eight years old, she and my father sent me to a Bible camp called Joy for Jesus. They thought it would be good for me to go away for a week and get a feel for independence, learn how to be on my own, and get to know some other kids. But I was not having it. I cried and cried, and begged to stay home. My mom says she felt terrible, that she hated watching me get on the bus all red-eyed, wet-faced. She remembers seeing me look out the back window, my cheeks pressed up against it, weeping.

When the bus pulled back into town the next week, she thought I'd be desperate to get home. But all I wanted to do was go back to camp. I begged the counselors to let me come back as soon as possible. They told Moms that I was one of the most connected kids they'd ever met. I was the only person who could get the white kids and the Black kids to play together, the city kids and the kids from the suburbs. They told her about how I helped other kids who were feeling homesick to loosen up and have fun. That I was constantly motivating everyone to get along and team up for flag football or sit at the same table or get out and run around first thing in the morning. Clearly, I have always been ET, the hip-hop preacher.

What I remember from that time was the distinct feeling of independence and freedom. For the first time in my life, I got a sense of who I was, apart from the rest of the world, and what I was capable of. When I got on the bus to go to a rural camp on Lake Huron a hundred and some miles away, I was terrified. First of all, Black people didn't go north for vacation. Traverse City, Port Huron, Mackinac Island—that's where the white folks went. You also have to remember that I grew up in an urban community. I saw what happened in scary movies when people went out to the country. They find Freddy Krueger out there and chain-saw massacres and people with hooks trying to carry you off to the woods. I wasn't interested in meeting the bogeyman or living primitively or sleeping in bunk beds on top of people I didn't know. I didn't have any interest in jumping in water where I couldn't see the bottom. The biggest body of water I'd ever been in was the Swim Mobile, an eighteen-wheeler that would roll around Detroit with a swimming pool on the back of it. I had never been in no lake before.

Before I got on that bus, I had always been within range of a family member. If it wasn't my mom, it was my aunties or grandmas, and, even running around Chicago, there was always some older cousin, Randy or Cory, around. You don't know what you don't know, and I didn't know how small my world was. When I got on the bus, it was the first time I stepped fully outside of my comfort zone, and I promise you, I was more apprehensive than I'd ever been in my life. But as soon as I looked around and saw the kids starting to have fun, I was in. Cats was telling jokes and I was good at jokes. So I got in on the "your mama" stuff, cracking people up, loving the attention. When we got to camp, I couldn't believe how beautiful it was. We went to Belle Isle growing up, a little place on the Detroit River, but I had never seen trees or green like that before. The Great Lakes were new to me—I had no idea Michigan had so much water. And making friends wasn't hard. I started hanging with a kid named José. I met all the camp counselors who were in college. I found a mother figure in the camp nurse and cook who spoke only Spanish. I befriended a counselor who looked like that artist dude Bob Ross and played guitar real soft around the campfire.

At that age, camp was the greatest thing that had ever happened to me. We played sports all day. We swam and fished and canoed. At night there were spooky stories and marshmallows around the campfire. We got points for making our beds and keeping things clean. There were three square meals a day and snacks on top of that. To an adult, seven days sounds short. But to a kid, it's a million years. It's also enough time in seclusion with new people to form bonds. I got close with everybody around me and I met Jesus for the first time. I didn't go to church growing up, so I didn't have too much understanding of Bible study or religion, but there I got a good feeling for how to pray and talk to God. And because I was so good at just being me, I got the opportunity to go back to that camp every summer for years as the transitional ambassador.

For the first time in my life, I got to feel what it was like to be in a position of leadership. For weeks at a time, I'd stay at camp and help kids figure out how to be away from home, calming their fears about new experiences and new people. I was doing readings and leading prayers. I was social to the max. For me, being in a new environment was a revelation. I got the first taste of what my superpower felt like. I had a knowledge that deep inside me, there was some sort of energy I could tap into. Just like when Superman first realized he could fly, or Spider-Man felt the webs come out of his wrists, when I was getting to know new people, helping them find their way in the world, I felt powerful.

But before I figured out how my superpower worked, before I understood how to use it or see it as a gift, sometimes it created more chaos than good. When you don't know how to channel your superpower, it can show up as harmful. A neglected superpower looks like dysfunction and leaves collateral damage in its wake.

When I was a kid in school, I was what teachers called "insubordinate." Every single report card I ever got had that word written on it somewhere: insubordinate, insubordinate, insubordinate. I didn't know what the term meant until later, but I get it now: I would do anything for attention. I liked to perform for my classmates, making jokes and showing off. I was always getting into trouble.

If a substitute teacher came in, I was running that joint, which is ironic, considering I ended up being a substitute teacher down in Huntsville, Alabama, later on. Because I was funny and I was a good talker, my boys would egg me on, encouraging me to make fun of vulnerable teachers.

The crazy thing is that when I was disrespecting teachers, I knew what was going to happen. I knew I would be sent to the principal's office. I knew my parents would get a call from the school. I knew in the car on the way home that I was going to get a whipping. And I knew that the punishment wasn't going to be worth my acting up. But I was an addict for attention. I was an addict for a laugh. I was an addict for affirmation.

When my gift was unchanneled, it showed up as impulsiveness. It showed up as me not thinking through my decisions. I ran away from home for good at sixteen without considering where I was going to sleep or how I was going to eat. I left without socks, underwear, or a toothbrush. It was March in Michigan, freezing rain every day. Who does that? Who leaves a good home to sleep on the streets?

When your gift isn't taken care of, it shows up like Batman running through walls. It shows up as destruction. You tear down relationships.

You tear down your world. It looks like wasted time and wasted opportunities. It looks like being homeless and getting kicked out of school.

All told, I changed schools seven times. I went to a Catholic school for a year, where the nuns paddled me and made me write the encyclopedia (I wasn't invited to come back). I went to Taft Middle School for a year, before switching over to Open House, an experimental charter school. I swapped high schools twice until the day I got kicked out for good for mouthing off to a teacher. Even though I was homeless, my mom still got called in. She was so disappointed in me. I remember sitting in the principal's office when she walked in and heard the news. It's still difficult for me to think about how disappointed she was in me that day.

Looking back, I can recall getting sent to school counselors. I didn't know it at the time, but they were doing evaluations to see if I had learning disabilities. They'd show me some ink splotches and ask what I saw and I'd say, "Ink." My reading comprehension was less than satisfactory. I just couldn't understand certain things like how the suffix -tion somehow got pronounced as "shun." Or how certain verbs acted differently from all the other verbs. I couldn't see punctuation or how the whole system of a sentence or a paragraph worked. When I read out loud, I read what I thought was there instead of what was actually on the page. Back in school, I could not sit still in a classroom. My body and my mind are simply not designed to sit anywhere for hours at a time. You invite me to a meeting, and I'll be at the table for fifteen minutes before I'm up, pacing around, and dipping out halfway through to take a call or a walk around the block. Now I understand that I'm dyslexic and have ADHD, but back then I was just bad at school and disruptive.

Today, we know that kids with these kinds of learning disabilities can overcompensate by becoming super relational or tapping into their intuition. They do things differently because they're forced to work outside the boundaries of traditional learning. Today schools have programs that play to those strengths and weaknesses with alternative teaching and learning methods. It makes sense that I became a speaker, that I compensated by building relationships and being social and working harder than anyone else to get ahead. It makes sense that I still don't do anything the conventional way. It's just not how my brain works. Even today, I work outside the box. Sometimes people don't appreciate that approach, but if you work outside the box and do it so well that it makes people see something a different way, you're using your superpower to its fullest.

To Activate Your Superpower, Tune Out the External World, and Tune In to You

I have always been attracted to people who know how to talk. When sports announcers came on the TV or news anchors hit the six o'clock news, I was there listening. So when I got to Detroit Center, Pastor Willis became my hero. There was something about his authority and charisma that was magnetic. When he stood up to speak, he knew how to grab everybody's attention with a phrase or a parable. He was famous for his sermons, and he was a wordsmith, coming up with sayings like "Don't be a jellyback!" Meaning: Don't be spineless. He would say, "All man, four squares," when talking about being a person who can take full responsibility for every part of their life. His military career bled over into his speaking style, and every sermon became a charge. He would do a countdown sometimes at the end of his sermons: "Ten! Nine! Eight! You got seven minutes and Noah is in the ark with his family, and they're about to shut the doors! Six! You gotta get in the ark! Don't get left behind!" He'd count all the way down to one, and by the end everybody was whooping and clapping.

Pastor Willis was aggressive, but not in a scary way. It reminded me of a lion protecting his pride. He would sit down all the young men in the church and ask us questions. "You going to school? How come you not in school? You got a job? How come you don't have a job? What do you need to do to take it to the next step?" If you were in Pastor Willis's church, you were part of his flock and he was looking after you. I loved this feeling of being protected, and I can see now that he was filling in for the sort of father figure I'd been so conflicted about. When Pastor Willis spoke, I felt like he was speaking to me. When he asked me questions, I felt seen.

As soon as I was in the door at Detroit Center, I started volunteering to read and lead prayers. If there was an opportunity to talk, I was on it. The congregation saw my enthusiasm and conviction, and they encouraged it. When it came time for our week of prayer, a period where, for seven days straight, the congregation got together, Pastor Willis invited me to do a sermon. His son would do Saturdays. My friend Bob did Fridays. Being the new guy, I got the Thursday spot.

Almost immediately I knew I was going to do a story called "Seven Ducks in Muddy Water." I'd picked it up from a minister at a revival in Atlanta we'd gone to earlier that year. A revival is a big tradition in our community. For a month, church members congregate under a tent every day to pray and sing and listen to sermons from the best preachers around. It's usually in the summer, and it can get intense with all that heat and all those people praying hard. Pastor Walter Pearson who led the Atlanta revival was a legend. The way I watched Pastor Pearson and Pastor Willis was like football fans watching Alvin Kamara run or Tom Brady throw a ball. The way they spoke was like Jordan dunking or Magic throwing a no-look pass. Their sermons were filled with verbal acrobatics. They mesmerized crowds and got standing ovations. I knew I wanted to be able to do that one day.

Pastor Pearson's version of the seven ducks story was taken from the book of Kings. An Aramean general goes to the prophet Elisha to see if there is a cure for his leprosy. Elisha tells the general that to get rid of his disease, he has to dip himself in the infamously murky waters of the river, seven times. The general doubts whether he should "duck" under the surface the full seven times, as he was prescribed. I always liked the stories that had a play on words or some creative way of making you think twice about what you were hearing.

I practiced my sermon for two weeks, pacing back and forth, up and down the street, in the church, in the shower. Because I wasn't living at home, I was spending a lot of time alone, so I had time to obsess about the nuances of my voice and cadence. It was a beautiful thing, having something to take my mind off the loneliness and get me focused. I practiced my crescendos and decrescendos the same way Michael Jackson and Aretha Franklin do in their music. If you've seen me speak, you know what I'm talking about. Sometimes I get real quiet, almost to a whisper, and you have to lean in to hear what I'm saying. Sometimes my voice gets real raspy when I'm trying to drive home a certain point. "You got to want to *succeed* as bad as you want to *breathe!*" These were things I'd picked up from Pastors Willis and Pearson intuitively, and I infused them into my own way of speaking.

When it came time to do the sermon, I got up in the sanctuary and looked around. I was nervous, but when it came down to it, I was like a fish in water. People were nodding and affirming me. The amens came and so did the clapping. For me, it felt like what people describe as an out-of-body experience. I was actively engaged, but another part of me was standing outside of all of it, taking it all in. I still feel that way today. I still get nervous when I stand up to speak, but once I'm up there, another part of me takes over, and I leave my body and get into a flow. The only way I know how to describe it is spiritual. A spirit moves through me and takes off running.

This is what a superpower feels like. You have something inside you that is big and powerful and delicate at the same time, and when you activate it, it's like watching Simone Biles do a floor routine or listening to one of Mozart's symphonies or witnessing Russell Westbrook rebound twenty times in a row or seeing Roger Federer make a backhand slice. It's pure poetry.

Once I was off and running at Detroit Center, I was almost like a ball hog when it came to speaking. Because I wasn't getting recognized academically or getting awards for playing sports, I found that the affirmation I was getting when I stood up and spoke nourished me in a way I'd never known. It was the first time I found myself activating my superpower and channeling it in a way that felt focused and healthy. Of course, I didn't realize at the time that you could get paid for speaking or that speaking professionally was a career option, but I knew I'd found something that I was good at and that I loved to do.

I'm lucky in this sense. I've had hardships with school and financials and plenty of other things in my life, but once I found my gift—my superpower—it was clear that I was moving toward some larger purpose. I found something to practice and to hold close and nurture.

But this wasn't always the case, and for many people it isn't immediately obvious what their specific gift is. We aren't all meant to be point guards in the NBA or quarterbacks in the NFL or actors in Hollywood blockbusters.

Sometimes our gifts reveal themselves over time. Sometimes our gifts are subtle or hidden. So how do you discover your superpower?

You cannot afford to live in potential for the rest of your life; at some point, you have to unleash the potential and make your move.

First, you have to be in touch with yourself. You need to be able to feel your gift—to understand what comes naturally to you or to see what you're innately attracted to. Maybe you love to look at paintings and photographs, and you can see color in a way that makes you feel something deep. Pay attention to this attraction. Maybe you have a knack for organization—you love making lists, and putting things on a calendar. That's a thing to note about yourself. Maybe when things are broken, you get a sense of satisfaction from putting them back together again, or assembling a piece of Ikea furniture when it comes out of the box. This is something to take stock of.

Finding your superpower is an active choice. It also requires active listening. You have to be ready to pick up on it and listen to it. It doesn't matter who you are: Everybody is drawn to something naturally. I believe that school is an important medium to advance your path through the world, but school cannot always help us figure out what we are good at. School has us focused on subjects—math, science, social studies—but not so much on how we interact with those subjects. In school, we engage with curriculum, but we aren't often encouraged to engage with how we process or what we feel about that curriculum. Even when we move from school into the professional world, the emphasis is put on the job or the position rather than the human in that job or position. It's cool to know what you want to study or what you want to be, but it's important to know who you are, too. It's important to think about what you're drawn to and examine why. It's important to explore why you're interested in a subject or a job.

In my case, I was always drawn to voices. If Howard Cosell with ABC Sports was on TV, I was standing there listening with my mouth open. Why is a kid like me from Detroit struck by Howard Cosell's nasally white-guy voice? If Bob Costas was announcing the Bulls, I was tuned in. Why was I feeling my man with his parted hair and his starched collars? As a kid, I loved listening to Barbara Walters and James Earl Jones, Maya Angelou and Stuart Scott. They each had something that just captivated me. When Pastor Willis got up, I was entranced. Even when I wasn't at church, I was thinking about the homily and the way it sounded. If I'd been more aware of myself back then, I would have asked myself why I loved listening to reporters and announcers. I might have spent some time thinking about what that made me feel and think.

In the same way that I have always naturally been attracted to speakers and their voices, I've also always wanted to help other people out. Mother Teresa was a celebrity to me. Nelson Mandela was an idol. Rosa Parks and Harriet Tubman were goddesses. I wanted to read everything about them, and I knew I wanted to help people, just as they did. If somebody I knew was having trouble at school or at camp, I would carry it with me, and wonder how they were doing. I have always been curious about how people feel, and if they're in need of something I can provide. Today, I know that not everybody leads with their emotions and intuition, but, as a kid, you don't know what you don't know. And I didn't know that I was different. Today, I pay attention to my natural inclinations and spend time getting in touch with them and developing them. Today, I tune in to me.

This is what's tricky about finding your superpower. We're each gifted with talents that come to us so naturally that we don't even notice they're talents. This is why finding your superpower is an internal exercise. It's about tapping into you and listening to what your inner voice and abilities are telling you. It's about tuning out the external world so you can hear what's going on inside yourself. This might mean spending a little more time alone and quiet. It might mean turning off the TV or putting your phone down and asking yourself some questions.

This is why I use the Flight Assessment when I work with companies and teams and players one-on-one. It's a tool to give people awareness of what's already there. It helps people to understand how and why they behave the way they do. It allows us to see clearly what we are good at and what we have to work on. There is a certain kind of peace in understanding that you don't have to be all things to all people. There's a comfort in knowing that you are you and that's enough.

You wanna shine like a diamond, you gotta get cut like a diamond.

When you're thinking about your superpower, ask yourself: What are the things you do that energize you? The things that after you've finished you feel that you could do for another hour or two or three? I can speak for five or six hours and not get tired. I can speak the way Venus can play tennis. I can speak the way Beethoven played the piano. I can speak the way Muhammad Ali could box. The way Michael Phelps swims. The way Kendrick Lamar raps. The way Kehinde Wiley paints. Speaking, for me, is like coffee. If I have the fuel, I can just go forever. What is the thing that you can get lost in? The thing that puts you in the flow or in the zone? Pay attention to the things that make you feel that time is irrelevant.

On the flip side, a superpower may be natural, but may not be an obvious career choice. Or you may be gifted at several things, and don't know how to choose among them. Growing up, I didn't know I could become a motivational speaker, and even into my twenties, I thought teaching and ministry were my main path. Being the number one speaker in the world just wasn't even an option in my mind. This lack of awareness was the same for the rapper Tobe Nwigwe.

Tobe had tracked me down about ten years ago. He had been watching my videos and got in touch to say that if I was ever in Houston he'd be happy to show me around town. So when I flew in one week, I took him up on it. He drove me all over the city, and if you've met Tobe, you know that he's a social creature, like me. He knows everybody and he's got that lion energy.

Come to find out, he had been a college football player who thought he was going to the NFL until he suffered an injury. After finishing college, he started a nonprofit dedicated to helping kids find their purpose in life. He had them doing skits, rapping onstage, putting together full productions, and getting them excited about their own gifts. My business partner CJ moved to Houston a few years later, and I connected him with Tobe. When CJ saw what the man was doing, he was floored and called me, telling me Tobe had to do something more with his gift. All credit to CJ, he sat Tobe down and told him that his calling was to make music and be a rapper. Tobe didn't totally believe him. He said he'd never written a song and didn't have any formal training, but CJ pressed it and convinced him that this was his path. Eventually, we helped Tobe get his career off the ground, but it would never have come to be if Tobe hadn't willed it into being. Like CJ and me, he's got that dog. He wants to work, and he took his gift and elevated it to the superpower you see today. Like us, he's a family man, a provider, and totally unconventional. Today, Erykah Badu, Michelle Obama, Dave Chappelle, Jill Scott, and P. Diddy all sing his praises. He's worked with Apple Music, Beyoncé, the NBA, Justin Timberlake, and has songs hitting the top of the charts every year.

What I love about Tobe's story is that he had to go through the process of becoming aware that he had a superpower, and once he became aware of that the power, he was willing to take a risk to see if his gift was real. He dedicated his life to pursuing the potential of his superpower with laser focus. This is key. Trying is key. How do you know what your power is if you don't try to use it? Your power cannot be discovered or tapped in to or channeled if you don't try. And sometimes you have to try again. And sometimes you have to try harder. Like any superpower, it has to be trained and honed and practiced in order for it to be useful.

Here's another thing I love about Tobe's story: I had no idea, but when Tobe picked me up from the airport that first day, he didn't even have a car. He had a buddy who worked at a rental car company who helped him out. Tobe, who grew up in the SWAT, one of Houston's roughest neighborhoods, is the inverse of a victim. He's always looking at what he *can* do. That boy puts himself in miracle territory. And he surrounds himself with people who will help him get to where he's headed. The lesson here is that if you want something bad enough, you'll find the people who will support you and you'll find the opportunity to get it. But first, you've got to know you want it and then you've got to want it bad.

Fall in Love with Your Superpower

Too often, our gifts can be obscured by a desire to conform to the mainstream. Conforming is what happens when we're tuned in to external voices rather than to our own intuition. Sometimes our gifts are not supported or nurtured by the people around us.

When I was very young, before I ever knew I was good at speaking, I had an affinity for the violin. In elementary school, when we were allowed to pick the instrument we wanted to play, I knew I wanted to play the violin. When you chose your instrument, the school lent it to you, so whenever I could, I took the violin home to practice. I just fell in love with the ritual of taking it out of its case, turning the pegs to tune it, and feeling the bow over the tension of the strings. When I listened to Earth, Wind & Fire or Stevie Wonder, I heard the strings. It was like they were speaking to me.

But when I began to share my excitement for the violin with my community, cats were like, "What? The violin? That's not sexy. That's not masculine." I started to question everything that I loved, and when I practiced, it was like I had the violin in one ear and everybody else in the other. And, unfortunately, everybody else was louder. I allowed the opinion of others to rob me of mastering a gift. I pushed away this thing that I innately felt drawn to and listened to the larger culture, which dictated what was and wasn't "acceptable." I let myself get bullied into abandoning my gift.

When you're tapped in to you, you know what your gift is and how to grow it. When you're tapped in to the world, it can distract you from being aware of or appreciating what your gift is. I listened to everyone else instead of what was inside me, and my gift went fallow. There's something about the idea of popularity that clouds the senses. It can feel easier to conform to the notion of what the rest of the world is doing than to go your own way and do something entirely new.

You don't reap what they sow. You reap what you sow.

When I was a kid, sports were what was cool for young men. If you didn't play football or basketball or run track, you were probably a nerd. There was an ideal that masculinity was equal to physical ability—running, catching, passing. Anything else—playing the violin, painting, studying—was not at the same level. To dream about the future was to imagine being rich and famous in the NBA or NFL, not to be a violin player in a symphony orchestra.

But it's funny—if you think about who society prizes, if you think about who we remember for centuries, it's the people who didn't conform. Society looks up to people who don't let themselves get bullied, who forge new paths where none existed before. But those paths are often not easy or popular. The value we place upon what is or isn't popular is a way of thinking. Nonconformity is often the result of an openness to difference and creativity. When I think about the superheroes I look up to, I think about people like Martin Luther King Jr. Frederick Douglass. Malcolm X. Harriet Tubman. W. E. B. Du Bois. Maya Angelou. Jackie Robinson. These are people for whom the path to success may not have been obvious or easy. Frederick Douglass was born into slavery. He had to learn to read and write in secret, and buy his very own freedom. Despite starting at less than zero, he became the greatest orator of his time. Malcolm X's father was killed by the Ku Klux Klan, and Malcolm went to jail for being a troublemaker, but eventually he transformed the very way we conceptualize Black power around the world. These are people who easily could have fallen prey to the paradigm of victim mentality, or who could have looked at and listened to popular opinion and gone nowhere. But once they tapped in to their superpower, they found themselves forging their own path despite the odds.

Even when other people don't recognize your gift, or the outside world doesn't validate it, you have to know with every fiber of your being that you are doing what is right for you. Trends come and go. Sometimes light skin is in. Sometimes dark skin is in. Sometimes it's short hair and sometimes it's long. You can't worry about what the world thinks is cool right now. You can only worry about you.

Today, I still put on violin music and listen to the great symphonies. I follow hip-hop artists who use the violin as a kind of language in their own work. I still love the sound of it, just as I used to, but I don't play anymore, and I wonder what might have been if I'd kept at it. I wonder if it was a superpower that I just never tapped in to.

You Are the Most Powerful When You Are the Most You

Of course, it took me some time to understand what my superpower was because, as a kid, I was always more tuned in to the external world than I was in to me. Affirmation and validation felt necessary for me to pick up on my gift. This got me into trouble in the classroom, and it also got me into trouble elsewhere. Being tuned in to validation from the outside world can be dangerous and lead us toward using our powers for the wrong reasons.

When I was a kid, I could run super fast. Honestly, I thought I was going to be in the NFL. Whenever we'd have to do our tests in PE class, my scores always put me among the fastest kids in the state. When I wasn't getting in trouble at school, I ran track and played football and I was always picked first for a team. I just loved running. And I also liked the thrill of getting chased.

For as long as I can remember, I was stealing stuff from stores. Penny candy. Video games. Clothes. I didn't even want the stuff. I just liked the adrenaline rush of seeing if I could outrun the cops. As a teenager, some of my homies tried to get me to sell dope, but I was good on that. However, I did sell the stuff I stole on the streets. If a friend wanted an outfit that cost $100 at the mall, I'd steal it and sell it to them for $75. And I was getting validated for it. The rush was exciting and I felt like I belonged when I showed up with all that expensive stuff people wanted to buy. For the longest time, it never bothered my conscience.

But when I started going to church, I got a bad feeling about stealing. I'd get uncomfortable thinking about what I was taking from other people. I didn't feel right sitting in front of Pastor Willis one day and sneaking out of a store with a pair of sneakers the next. So one afternoon, after getting away with a whole bunch of stuff from a department store at the Somerset Mall, I decided to go back and turn myself in. I knew that if I didn't get caught, I'd just keep doing it. I told my buddy who had the getaway car to go home because I was going to jail. He thought I was crazy, but I knew it's what I had to do. When I went back into the store, I acted real shady, and started walking out with some piece of clothing or a hat. And of course, a salesperson saw me and called me out.

I'll never forget it. It was cosmic or something, but my father's cousin who was like my auntie was there when it happened. She watched me get put in cuffs by the mall cops, and get walked to the back of the store like a criminal. She didn't say anything, but she had a look in her eye, and two days later, my whole family knew. My mom was so hurt, and I was more embarrassed than I'd ever been.

I don't let go of people, I outgrow them.

As with playing the violin, outside validation was detrimental to developing my gifts. Because I wasn't aware of my gifts, I wasn't able to listen to myself. Unfortunately for me, I needed external affirmation to get tuned in to myself. So, when I finally surrounded myself with people who were supportive of my natural abilities in a healthy way, a light came on. I should have realized that I was interested in speaking, but I didn't know it until I got the opportunity. When Pastor Willis and my church community saw my superpower, they began to give me opportunities to use it and try it out. And I could finally feel within myself that this was the gift I should focus on. I finally felt like me.

Nobody can be more you than you. When you're tapped in to your superpower, you are fully in yourself and your gifts. You're the most powerful when you are you.

The last step to discovering your superpower after recognizing it is falling in love with it. You have to get to know every angle of it. You have to get obsessed with it. You have to get intimate with your gift. It should feel like a romantic relationship. You can't be number one in the world if you aren't obsessed with your gift. You can't be the best at what you do if you don't honor your gift. If you're going to contribute to your field or advance the game or get mentioned with the greats before you, you have to be dedicated to getting up every morning and taking care of it. Like any relationship that's worthwhile, your relationship with your gift requires work. If you get complacent and don't work at it, your gift will go fallow. Even if you are naturally good at what you do, that is not enough. You have to work at it and you have to want more.

There are plenty of people who, with very little instruction, can hear a song, pick up a guitar, and play. But unless they get into their gift and practice, they're never going to play like Jimi Hendrix. Plenty of people can open their mouths and sing beautifully. But if they don't get obsessed with the gift of it, they're never going to get to Beyoncé-level. Steph Curry was born with the ability to throw and sprint, but if he hadn't worked at it and gotten consumed by it, he wouldn't be the NBA legend he's become. Serena Williams was always going to be able to smash a tennis ball, but had she not put in the grueling hours of somebody who wants to win, she wouldn't have the accuracy or grace she shows up with on the court today.

I wake up every day in love with my gift. It still feels like an intimate relationship. I still get butterflies when I'm about to go onstage. I honor the people who came before me. I honor the fact that I have a gift. Of course, the money is nice, but money only showed up after I got obsessed with my superpower. The tangible fruits of my labor only came after I began channeling my power toward my path of purpose.

The Work

1. What are you naturally good at? What are you naturally attracted to? Make a list of these things, big and small.

2. Are you aware of how you can channel these natural inclinations? How can you become more aware of them? Can you visualize one or more of these things becoming a superpower?

3. What could your superpower look like if you spent time with it and worked to get it to a place of excellence?

4. What might it look like when it isn't channeled? How does it show up and what does that feel like?

5. What can you do to take care of your superpower and advance it, every day and in the long run? How can you further it and practice it a little bit each day?

Challenge: Spend time with yourself. Find a quiet place, and spend twenty or thirty minutes every day making notes or talking to yourself about what you love and are good at or are attracted to. Find some clarity about how you want to cultivate your gifts and where you want to go with them. Create a list of ideas about how you can begin activating your superpower in ways big and small. What can you do each day? What can you do over the course of the next month or year? How can you fall more in love with your superpower? Make a list of books, programs, documentaries, people, or places that will inspire you to activate your gifts. Make a decision to wake up every day and use your gift in some way.

CHAPTER

4

What's Your Why?

WHEN YOU FIND YOUR WHY, YOU CAN TAKE YOUR SUPERPOWER AND YOUR LIFE TO THE NEXT LEVEL.

Your why is what takes your superpower to the next level. Your why is the thing that keeps you going. Your why is what pushes you forward. Your why is what gives you something to wake up for. The whole reason I am where I am today is because of my wife Dede. She was the person who helped me see that there was more in front of me than I'd let myself imagine. She was the person who helped me find me. She was the person who helped me uncover my reasons for moving through the world.

We'd been together for a little over a year when she called me over to her house one day in April. I had been kicked out of high school and she was finishing up her senior year. Her mom wasn't home and she was acting weird. Very focused and kind of serious. We sat down on the porch and she said she needed to ask me something.

"Do you love me?" she said. "Yeah, I love you," I told her. But then she challenged it. "But do you *love me* love me?" And I answered her, "Of course I love you." She asked me if I loved her enough to change my life, to get off the streets and make a decision to do something bigger. When I asked her what she meant, she told me she'd gotten into Oakwood College (it has since become Oakwood University) and that she was going to Huntsville, Alabama, in the fall. Then she asked me if I would think about going with her, and if I might be able to see leaving Detroit as the beginning of something more. I may not have thought about it this way, but when I look back now, this is the first time I ever identified what my "why" in life was: to be with Dede and to make her happy.

I had never thought about what was coming next. I had never thought about leaving Detroit or what my life could look like if I finished school. It had just never crossed my mind. I didn't have a place to live. How was I going to imagine where I was going to live in ten years? When I thought about leaving the city with Dede, I felt something totally new. I felt hope. It was like a fire was lit underneath me. I knew I couldn't lose this person who had taken me in when I had nothing. Part of what attracted me to her was that she was everything I wasn't. She was laser-focused. She was a decision maker. She had a plan and a direction. She was going places. And if she left, I was going nowhere without her. I looked around and saw my life for what it was. I was a high school dropout, living on the streets of Detroit with no future to speak of. What was I going to do? Keep living out of my car, working at McDonald's?

If I was going to college in the fall, the first thing I had to do was get my GED. I called Pastor Willis, who helped set me up in night school, where I started taking GED classes. For me, that test meant everything. My whole future hung on it. As I studied, the test became a symbol of power and possibility. I would get butterflies whenever I opened my books, especially when I thought about the writing and reading comprehension sections. Some days I would get a concept right away, and sometimes it would take me several days to understand something like conjugation or antecedents. But, the whole time, I had a sense of energy and a desire to love school I'd never had before.

The week before the test, I couldn't sleep at all. I played out in my head all the scenarios of what could happen. What would it mean if I didn't pass? Dede would leave for Alabama without me, and I'd still be in Detroit. My rock would be gone and everything would fall apart. If I passed, what did it mean that I would be going somewhere totally different, starting a whole new life?

After I finished the test, I closed the booklet, put down my pencil, and didn't know how to feel. I knew I'd done okay, but I wasn't sure if it was enough to put me over the line. The first part of the GED is graded locally, but the writing section is sent to Washington, DC, for evaluation, so I had to wait a few weeks before I would know the results. At the time, I was using my boy Bob's mom's house as an address, so I would go over there every day to see if it was in the mailbox. The day the results finally arrived it was raining. I stood on the porch, holding the letter in my hand, thinking about the fact that my whole life was wrapped up in this one little envelope. Part of me wanted to look at it and part of me didn't. After three or four minutes, I finally ripped it open and unfolded the piece of paper. I'd passed. I had my GED. I felt like I had my ticket, and I was at peace. I got on my bike and rode over to show Dede.

One of the many beautiful things about my church, Detroit Center, was that it was a direct pipeline to Oakwood College, which was founded by Seventh-Day Adventists. Every young person who went to Detroit Center knew that if they wanted to and worked hard enough, they had an inroad to Oakwood, part of the HBCU (Historically Black College and University) system. When I got in, it was by the grace of Pastor Willis who promised me if I got the GED, he'd figure it out.

I arrived at Oakwood in 1989 without any study or research skills and no real idea of what I wanted to do. I got a grant, a scholarship, and had help from the school's donors to get me started. The rest I'd have to pay for with student loans. My dorm, Cunningham Hall, was the first consistent place I'd lived in two years. I loved living there, making pancakes in the communal kitchen, chopping it up with other kids, hanging out in the common rooms or halls. But above everything else, I was there for Dede.

When you take care of something good, that something good takes care of you.

The summer after our freshman year, I knew I could only go back to Oakwood if it was official. A few weeks before we were supposed to go back to school, I took Dede out to TGI Friday's. After we sat down and ordered, I told her that I wanted to be with her forever. I told her that I couldn't see myself without her, that I didn't want to miss out on being with someone who had given me something to live for. If I was going back to Oakwood, I was going back as her husband. So, a few weeks later, we went off and eloped. We got married at a courthouse in Toledo, Ohio, on August 23, 1990. It cost $25—cheaper than in Detroit—and we were both nineteen. We wore matching shorts sets, black with purple and yellow paisley. We had a stranger as our witness.

This was impulsive—typical me. I didn't know if I was going to be able to provide for us or where we were going to live or how to plan for a life together, I just knew I wanted to be with Dede. When our parents found out, they were pissed. Dede's mom especially, and I can't blame her. Who wants a homeless guy dating their daughter and riding her coattails to college? My mom was more worried for Dede than she was for me, which was also fair. But, luckily, Dede knew what she was doing. And I knew I was doing everything for Dede.

My why then and now is her.

Up until Oakwood, school had always been about recess and socializing for me. When I started taking classes, I did okay in electives, but in requirements like English and high-level biology, I struggled. Over the course of my sophomore year, my GPA declined and by junior year I was on academic probation. Where I'm from, nobody in my family went to college. My grandmothers didn't make it through high school. My biological father never completed high school, and my mom barely graduated after the administration found out she was pregnant. (Later she went on to get her degree in business administration at Davenport.) In my family, there wasn't a culture of keeping up your grades or checking in to make sure that you were going to class or on the path to graduation. So I just did what I wanted to do. Even Dede wasn't tripping on the fact that school wasn't my thing.

Around the time that my grades were going down, I got involved in Oakwood's GED outreach program. The school's motto was ENTER TO LEARN. DEPART TO SERVE, and a big part of campus culture was volunteer work. After church on Sundays, the pastor would lead us out to buses where we'd line up for sack lunches and get taken out into the community to work at the hospital or the nursing home. I loved working at those places, but I had a burning desire to do something more, so I jumped into the GED program. It was probably because I'd gotten a GED myself that it felt natural to me to want to help other kids puzzle through it. I saw myself in those kids from the projects in Huntsville and innately felt that I knew how to help them.

Huntsville's a weird place. It's in the middle of nowhere, so when you drive in you're coming through real rural territory. Cotton fields for miles. Every blue moon, I'd get out of the car and walk out into the middle of one of those fields. I'd put my hands out to touch the sticky stalks and white fluff. I would think about all the people who'd worked in those fields less than a century before and how I was connected to them. It felt like a ghost story.

The city of Huntsville itself is a mix of contradictions. It's rich and poor. Black and white. Stuck in antebellum days and full of modernity. NASA and Teledyne Brown and Boeing are all based there. The Redstone Arsenal, a missile-testing and space project base, is there, too. Huntsville is progressive and productive, but it's also segregated. There were four massive projects that housed the majority of the Black population, and they always looked threadbare. Clotheslines were strung up out of people's windows, little front and back yards without much grass. It wasn't as rough as Detroit or Chicago, but it wasn't beautiful. A lot of the kids I taught in the GED program came from these projects, and in their living rooms, I felt right at home.

When I started teaching the GED class, I studied the math and reading comprehension in a different way than when I first learned them, looking for all the ways a kid might understand the test questions. A lot of teachers, it seemed, couldn't help these kids with the GED because they couldn't make it practical. The way I thought about it combined psychology and practice. I would go home, take the test over and over again, and then read through personal development books like Dale Carnegie's *How to Win Friends and Influence People*, Og Mandino's *Greatest Salesman in the World*, and Norman Vincent Peale's *The Power of Positive Thinking*. Then I'd bring those books and read excerpts I thought might motivate the kids and get them to think critically.

In class, I'd spend half the time talking to them about the right mind-set to get them to understand why school is valuable and the other half of the class focusing on instruction. Sometimes I'd read Dennis Kimbro's *Daily Motivations* or *Think and Grow Rich*, and ask them how those ideas applied to them. In the beginning of class, I'd play hip-hop to pump them up and then classical music when they got down to serious work. Every thirty minutes, I had them get up and move around, and sometimes when they were taking tests I'd try to distract them to get them to practice staying focused. I had them visualize getting their results in the mail, seeing their scores, and feeling what kind of change that could bring to their lives. I challenged them to think about the futures they were moving toward, and ask them to consider the reasons behind their progress.

There's a stereotype against kids who don't finish school. It's easy to think they're dumb and lazy and don't have a future. But what I saw when I looked at these kids was a misunderstanding of the value of learning. I come from a place where it's enough to have a high school diploma or a GED to go and get a good blue-collar job. There's a disconnect between the value of work and the value of learning. There's also often a fundamental disconnect between what we do in the world and why we do it. If we understand *why* we're doing what we're doing, the *what* of the doing becomes more effective, more powerful, and attracts more opportunity.

Your overarching why is something very deep beyond tangible things—providing for your spouse and your kids, maintaining your health—and it's supported by an array of values that are natural to you. The Flight Assessment measures these values and puts into perspective what's driving your behavior. I value altruism, which means I'm always concerned about other people's needs and what I can do to help them. I also value individualism, meaning I have a deep sense of independence and self-confidence. Of course, this all makes sense. I have always treated ministry and volunteering like a career rather than an extracurricular activity. And after finding out about my biological father, I vowed to never let anyone have control over my decisions again. These values are aligned with my why—taking care of my family, looking out for my community, and giving back to my ministry.

Your Why Is Your Reason behind the Reason

By 1998, I was still working at the GED program and I'd become a permanent substitute teacher at Oakwood Academy, the high school associated with the university. Ironically, I had dropped out of college. I couldn't see it at the time, but there was a paradox between my having left school and my helping other people get through school. (Sometimes my altruism gets in the way of my helping me first.) Oakwood isn't a big place, so sports are secondary to academics. There's a certain status to being able to say you graduated from Oakwood. It means something, especially in the Black and Seventh-Day Adventist community.

But I was getting validation from other places. I'd started traveling with a lobbyist, Lamar Higgins, who promoted gun-buyback programs and voter registration. I was getting opportunities to give speeches introducing the mayor of Huntsville and the governor of Alabama. I was going to city council meetings and getting involved with the school board. I was on morning talk shows and in the paper, and it seemed like everybody knew who I was. All of that felt good, but I still didn't have a clear understanding of what the overarching goal behind it was. Where was I going and why? Even though I was working hard, I was still probably operating at 60 or 70 percent of my capacity.

What really changed everything was having our first child. I was twenty-four. Dede and I had been married for five years, and we both felt ready. Or as ready as we could be. Dede had finished nursing school by then and had a good job at Huntsville Hospital. I'd read all the books, and we had been taking care of our teenage neighbor's twin infant daughters, Brooke and Brianna, loving them as if they were our own. Feeding them, changing their diapers, putting them down for naps.

Jalin was born near midnight on July 20, 1995. When he came into the world, it was the first time Dede and I felt we had something that was ours. Up until then, we had goals that supported each other, but they were still independent of a unified vision on a single path. In the first moments that we held him, we became a family, and almost immediately I started to see the world with different eyes. It was spooky. That day, I became a provider and a protector on a whole different level. I realized that somebody else was going to be affected by my decisions

91

beyond just myself. I also saw my family's generational pattern clearly for what it was. The men in my family had been absent and the expectations placed upon them nonexistent. When I cut the umbilical cord between Dede and Jalin, I looked at him, helpless and tiny, and felt the possibilities in the world shifting. I could change something that was deeper than my own future.

This is the first time I truly understood my why. Your why is the reason behind the reason. You may want to get that job, but *why* do you want that job? Is it so you can make some extra cash to get yourself back to school? Is it to help support your parents, who are struggling with their own health issues? Is it to ensure that you have a safe place to sleep at night and food on the table? You can be doing something and working hard, but unless you've identified the reason you're doing something—the pure essence of why, exactly, you're grinding—the grind is going to be different. The architecture built on top of your blueprint will be executed differently. When Jalin was born, I finally identified where I was going and why.

What changed when I found my why? My time for play was over. I needed to cut out distractions. I stopped playing video games and sitting around playing cards, shooting the breeze. I went back to my counselors at Oakwood and begged them to let me back into school. I got laser-focused. With a regular light, you can illuminate your house, but with a laser, you can do surgery, you can cut diamonds. When Jalin was born, I got extremely serious about what was coming next. Because it wasn't just my life anymore. It was Jalin's life, too.

Over the course of your life, your why will change and shift and grow. It will become layered and deepen. And as your why shifts, so will your intensity. The reciprocal results will manifest in your professional and personal growth in ways you might not have imagined. Since Jalin was born, and eventually my daughter Jayda, my why has become more and more focused on my family. I feel a deep desire to protect and provide for them. To give them stability and build a legacy they can have when I'm gone from this world. And over the years, my why has, at points, become more focused and intense.

My why has become more layered as well. I feel a calling to take care of my community. CJ tells me I've got a Moses complex, but I promise you, this feeling is real. I think it has a lot to do with coming from a community of people who were enslaved and still experience inequality and inequity because of this history. I feel that I have a responsibility to shepherd them to protection and safety. I feel that whatever I do in the world must be a blessing to my people. As an African American man, I feel that I need to put my people on my back. My money is not just my money. It's my community's money. My influence is not just my influence. It is my community's influence. So many athletes I work with didn't just start playing basketball or football because they liked it, but because they thought it was the only way they would get out of the hood and the only way to get their mama a car and a house. Today, my why is partly about carrying my people further than they would go on their own.

My why is about my ministry, too. As a pastor, I always feel a desire to bless the people who have blessed me. Sometimes I feel a certain amount of pressure from the religious community to evangelize, but religion and spirituality are so personal that I'd rather let people discover it for themselves and come along when they're ready. I think this is what keeps people coming back to my ministry. I'm not about pressuring or building a church the traditional way. For so long, religion has been about building the institutions behind the church, constantly asking people to give up their money and their lives. For so long, it's been unequal. In my ministry, we try to give back more than anyone gives us. We put kids through college, help people get their credit scores up and buy cars, do marriage counseling, attend graduations and births and funerals. My why requires of me to always give more than I receive.

Your Why Is beyond the Extrinsic

It's possible that your why will not be obvious. It's possibly you'll struggle with finding your why, but, I promise you, it's necessary. Ironically, professional athletes have the most difficult time with this. I always tell them that the worst and best thing that ever happened to them is making it to the league. I deal with this when talking to rookies all the time. Making it to the league is anticlimactic. As children, their why *is* the league. All their goals are based on getting into the league. The structure of their lives is set up to maximize their talents and their time so that the league can stay in sight. Early morning weight lifting, special diets, after-school conditioning, sleep schedules—all of it is built around the goal of being drafted. You give up the extracurriculars most young people get to experience—video games, junk food, sleeping in, partying—all for the dream of going pro.

Now imagine getting into the league at nineteen, twenty, twenty-one years old. You're a multimillionaire. You're in the same spaces with LeBron and Tom Brady and Serena Williams. Your mom can buy the house she always wanted. She's got a car. You've got a house and a car. You've got a personal chef and can afford shoes and clothes and haircuts. Your outside desires are fulfilled. You've achieved the dream. But the problem is you aren't prepared for the league itself. Or for what comes after.

When you focus on the internal, the external fades away.

When your desires are extrinsic—a job, a house, a car, a handbag—your energy is different. You can be working hard, but you're not going to be working as hard as you might for an intangible reason. Extrinsic fuel is fundamentally different from intrinsic fuel. There are people who can't run a mile but who run marathons for a cause. If you're doing something for your kids or your wife instead of that new watch, your energy is different. Your why is the fuel for your superpower. It's what propels you along the path of purpose.

We all know what *NFL* stands for: "Not for long." Other sports are more forgiving, but the fact is that athletes are dependent upon their body. And the body is an ephemeral vessel. No matter who you are, you have to have goals beyond your body. This is why we mortals save for retirement. This is why we make ten- and fifteen- and twenty-year plans. This is vital for athletes who work their bodies for our entertainment. It's rare for somebody to make it into their late thirties playing the game. I often ask my players: What age do you want to die? Eighty? Ninety? That's fifty or sixty more years beyond the game. That's two more lifetimes than they've even imagined yet. What I tell them is that they must find their why beyond the game to keep playing the game.

Every year, I talk to the NBA rookies before the season starts. It's usually in a hotel somewhere in Jersey and when you walk in, you see all these massive men walking around in their sweats, looking for the buffet, eyeing each other. But when you look closer, you can see they're really just kids. Some of them don't even have facial hair coming in yet. These are the most elite athletes in the world, worth billions of dollars all together, entire corporations and advertising strategies and marketing budgets leveraged in their names, and many of them are barely out of adolescence. Some of them already have a swagger and a sense of entitlement that comes with the knowledge of new wealth or status. Some of them are humble and terrified and experiencing impostor syndrome—feeling intimidated or that they're not enough or that they're not fitting into someone else's paradigm.

To level the playing field and get their attention, I get up and talk about their futures and their responsibilities in terms of history. I tell them to look around the room, look at each other, and then think about what their futures would have looked like 200 years ago, 150 years ago. I ask them what they would have been in the world. The stark fact is, many of them would have been enslaved, working in fields, toiling at somebody's big house with no future to speak of. Then I ask them to think about what Martin Luther King Jr. would have done with the money they're making today. What Malcolm X would have done with it. What Harriet Tubman would have done with $10 million, $30 million, $50 million contracts. When I ask these questions, what I want them to do is look beyond their immediate career to what is coming next. The game is temporary. Their physical strength is temporary. But their legacy is lasting. If you're working for a legacy or to uplift a generation or to change the world, the way you perform in the world will be different. The results of your work will be different.

There are certain things in life that money can't pay for.

When I think about individuals finding a why beyond the immediate future, I think about Chris Paul. Here's a man who made it to the NBA at nineteen, has played for five teams, been in the Olympics twice, and been an eleven-time All-Star. CP3 is a legend because he's talented, but also because he knows he's working for something beyond each game. With his money and talents, he's made it his responsibility to bring opportunity to kids all over the country with leadership camps set up in each city he's ever played for. The head of the NBA Players Association, CP3 is not only a living example of what leadership can look like, but he's actively created opportunities for kids who might not have had them to understand what their why and purpose might be.

I think about Demario Davis, a linebacker for the New Orleans Saints who, after getting into trouble, found his footing and started a nonprofit that works with youth all over the world. He's politically active. He has a purpose beyond playing football. I think about Devon Still, a defensive end for the Cincinnati Bengals, who found out that his four-year-old daughter Leah had stage 4 neuroblastoma, a form of cancer, and even though he'd been recently injured and had surgery, he stayed by her side in the hospital for three weeks straight. He shaved his head and put his football career on hold. What's incredible about Devon's story is that his why resonated with the world. His team allowed him to go on leave, and raised $400,000 for pediatric cancer research at the Cincinnati Children's Hospital. Teams all over the NFL came out to support Devon and Leah. Because his why deepened and became such a strong part of his story and his identity, the world showed up and met him in his why.

The first time I ever talked about the concept of a why was when I spoke to the Miami Dolphins in 2012. I told them the story about Kevin Durant's jersey number. Up until he played for the Nets, Durant wore number 35. And when he got out on the court, he did something that should have terrified his opponents. He touched the numbers on the front of the jersey. He touched the numbers on the back of his jersey and then he pointed at the sky. He wore number 35 to honor his youth basketball coach Charles Craig, who died when he was 35, killed by four gunshot wounds in a parking lot. Kevin Durant played his games for that man. Durant was formidable not only because he was good, but because he had a why.

Today, "What's your why?" has become a staple in sports. It's been capitalized on by big brands to market a sense of intensity and grit. But the whole point of a why is always bigger than money and tangible things. A why is always about moving through your purpose toward something bigger than yourself.

Your Why Can Be Found by Looking Within

How do you uncover a why for yourself? In the same way that you find your superpower: By sitting with yourself, by quieting the external noise, you find your why through some serious alone time. Weird as it might sound, I found my why in the loneliness of being homeless. When I was at the crib, I would wake up to the sound of the coffeepot brewing or my mom making breakfast. I'd go outside and run up and down the block just to see who would play with me. I was around people all the time because I thought I needed constant stimulation. I thought I needed to be constantly moving and doing and talking.

Looking back, I can see that in forcing myself to be alone—to acclimate to the emptiness of an abandoned building, the unfamiliar sounds beyond the house I grew up in—I started to listen to myself and use my gut to move toward things I was drawn to. I gravitated toward working. Even though I didn't have a home, I knew how to get a job. I'd been working since I was twelve, starting with a two-block paper route along Braile and Patton. I knew all my customers, how much they owed me, who got the Sunday paper that cost an extra 75 cents. I liked working and it gave me structure and focus, and when I was homeless, it gave me a reason to show up.

Your why is what you think about underneath everything else. If you're working, you're thinking about it. If you're on vacation, you're thinking about it. It's something that follows you all around and taps on your shoulder when you're not paying attention to it. In all that time alone on the streets, I thought about all the things I was missing. And all those things revolved around family. Even though I was still mad at my mom, I missed her fiercely. I missed my sister Jeneco and my aunties and my grandmas. I wondered how big my two-year old sister Malori was getting. I thought about Dede all the time, and wondered what she was doing when we weren't together. And, of course, I thought about my new family at the church, and my responsibility to the community there.

Even back then, my why was about family. When I found Dede, she drew the lines of what a future family could look like. When Jalin was born, he shaded in all the lines, and when my daughter Jayda came along three years later, she deepened the color of it all. Today, I need to make sure my mom is provided for. I need to make sure she has a car and a house and vacations. Even now, if I haven't called my mom in a day or two, something doesn't sit right in my spirit. My why, whether I said it out loud or not, has always been about being part of and providing for a family.

Here's what's scary: Finding your why can be painful. Some of us suppress our why so we can keep conforming to the world's standards. And in suppressing our why, we deny our superpower and our purpose.

I used to get worried that my boys would be tripping on the fact that I was getting my GED and applying to college. I'd hear them in my head: "Oh, you on that college thing? You ain't even college material." But, thankfully, I had the balance of sitting with myself and listening to my voice instead of theirs. I spent a lot of time by myself in the dark, thinking dark things, being paranoid, feeling disconnected from everyone and everything around me. But as soon as I reconnected to myself, I began to reconnect with the world and find the deeper layers of my why through the desire to continue those connections. Whether I knew it or not, I was seeking a why.

The Work

1. What are your thoughts drawn toward naturally when you aren't working or playing? Where do you see yourself and who do you see yourself with when you imagine happiness?

2. What do you wake up in the morning for? Who do you wake up in the morning for? Who is it you want to see most? Who do you feel you don't want to live without? Who takes care of you and who do you take care of? Who do you want to take care of?

3. Who do you want to spend your future with? Friends, family, kids, a spouse? What does that future look like? What has shaped that vision? Who has shaped it? Is it what *you* want?

Challenge: Think about your extrinsic desires. What are the literal things you want? Now look behind that: Why do you want those things? Look toward your intrinsic desires. The things you want to achieve. Your dreams. The people you want to spend time with. The legacy you want to create. Think about *why* you want these things. Why do you want to achieve anything? Why do you dream? Who do you want to achieve for and dream with? Sort through these answers and you will begin to see a pattern. Your why will begin to emerge. Now take that why and write it on a Post-it and put it somewhere you will see it every day. And, every day, wake up, look at it, and remind yourself that this is why you are doing what you are doing today to the best of your ability.

CHAPTER

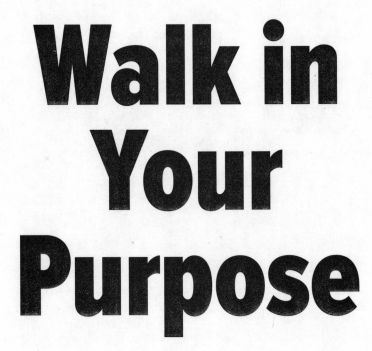

Walk in Your Purpose

MOVING THROUGH THE AWARENESS OF YOUR GIFTS IS WALKING IN YOUR PURPOSE.

Once you've activated your superpower and identified your why, you can begin moving in this awareness. You can start looking outside yourself to see what other people need from you. You can take your self-knowledge and apply your gifts to the people and places who need it most. Becoming aware is the first step. Moving through that awareness is walking in your purpose. Walking in your purpose is living up to your fullest potential and using your gifts every day. The Bible says that your gifts will make room for you. The path of purpose is that room.

Oakwood was the first place I started to walk along my own path of purpose with real direction. At Detroit Center, I got a taste of what it was like to speak publicly—the empowerment it made me feel, the joy it brought me to stand up and give a message. At Oakwood I got deeper into that feeling and that space. I'm not exactly sure how or why, but in my first week of school I found out I had been given the responsibility of speaking at the first convocation of the year. It was as if my gift had opened up the opportunity and begun unfolding to make room for me.

Soon after, at freshman orientation, I met some of my first friends outside of Detroit, Irvin Daphnis and Melvyn Tres Hayden III. Irvin was a first-generation Haitian American who grew up in Miami. He was six feet tall, thin, and dark. He was always in African garments, wearing a dashiki, sporting the 'fro. He was all about repping African heritage and he came from a background of heavy organizing as the president of the youth division of the Urban League. Tres, on the other hand, was a zealot for church. All Jesus all the time. His dad was a Seventh-Day Adventist preacher, so he studied the Bible, went to every service, fasted, prayed, and was involved in every campus group—Men of Discipline, Gamma Si Gamma, the choir Dynamic Praise. Tres's whole family had gone to Oakwood, and everybody knew and loved him. I was in all the same programs with Irv and Tres, and we got close. We started to feel like there was a larger sense of purpose drawing us together. When we got together we were like firecrackers.

This was 1989. This was the era when Rodney King was assaulted by police in Los Angeles. This was the time of Spike Lee's *Do the Right Thing* and *School Daze*. This was just after the era of Governor George Wallace's segregationist policies in Alabama. When you're a young Black man in America, there's always something going on: Fourteen-year-old Emmett Till getting lynched in 1955, David Duke reviving the KKK in Louisiana in the 1970s, George Floyd's murder in Minneapolis in 2020. When we got to school, we started to hear about our heritage in full for the first time and connect all the pieces of the puzzle. We saw the footprints of slavery all over American history. We read about the crops we sowed and the cities we built with our own hands. We talked about Africa and our ancestors who were kings and queens. We learned that the Sphinx and the Pyramids and the university at Timbuktu were created by our people. That we conceptualized time and made the world's first clocks. We discovered that we had history and lineage that went far beyond Jamestown and Comfort Point and Charleston and New Orleans. When I went to school in Detroit, these things just weren't taught to us.

Irv, Tres, and I felt that we needed to share what we were feeling and all the knowledge we were soaking up. We felt that the spirit of Harriet Tubman and Jesse Jackson and Muhammad Ali and Nelson Mandela had leapt into us, and we were obliged to carry on their work. So, we went on a seven-day fast, no food, just water. And at the end of it, we knew we should form some sort of ministry. I felt strongly that it should feel nonintrusive and give people the choice to come in and listen, stay awhile, or to pass by if it wasn't their thing. This is how Bell Tower Ministry was born.

The Oakwood campus is beautiful. Green, grassy, lined with massive oak trees. It was built to be a Black school by the white organization behind the Seventh-Day Adventist Church. There isn't a main road that passes by the campus. There's one little road in and the same little road out. It's isolated from the rest of Huntsville. This was by design—partly to keep students in, to keep them safe, and to keep anyone out whose intentions weren't good. It wasn't uncommon to see pickup trucks outside the city with a Confederate flag in their back windows, and you knew if you were driving to Oakwood, you didn't stop for gas in any of the small towns on its outskirts. When you got to campus, the school felt like a little world unto itself.

When we thought about where to set Bell Tower up, it was obvious: Right in the middle of campus is an actual bell tower that everyone had to pass on their way to class or the dorms or the cafeteria. The question of when seemed pretty obvious, too. At Oakwood, every Wednesday night there's a major chapel service. On Fridays the Adventist Youth Society meets, and on Saturday there's an all-campus service. So every Tuesday, Thursday, and Sunday, in the evenings, Irv, Tres, and I went and stood at the Bell Tower and started giving messages.

At first, I was the host and organizer. I'd pass out flyers in the dorms, and spread the word. I'd introduce whoever was speaking at the Bell, and pull the details together. Occasionally, I'd give a little talk, but mostly I was the emcee. We didn't have microphones. We didn't have chairs or soapboxes to stand on. We just got out there and did our thing. The first time I stood up at Bell Tower to speak, it was chilly outside and drizzling. It was dark, but we were near a light pole, so people could see us out there, our shadows moving big around us. I probably spoke for fifteen or twenty minutes about whatever I was on at the time—spirituality, making better decisions. I don't know—I was a rookie. But, little by little, people started to hover, and they hung around. I realized that they were there watching me, nothing forcing them to be there or stick around.

Become Aware, Then Become You

Becoming aware was the first step to understanding my purpose. After Detroit Center, I knew I had an ability to speak in public. I knew I was attracted to it. When I found other people who were interested in the same things and we supported each other in our collective interest, I became more grounded in myself, and my purpose began to flourish. I began to see a path I could take with intention. You don't get on an airplane or get into a car with nowhere to go. You get in knowing you have a journey and a destination. This is what getting onto the path of purpose feels like—starting an intentional journey.

Looking back, I can see the birth of Bell Tower very clearly as the moment when I started to transition into a man. Part of this had to do with becoming aware of what it means to grow up Black in America. It was also about understanding that the world was so much bigger than just me. At Oakwood, there were kids from all over—Toronto and England, Boston and California. And they all had different accents and different styles. Detroit was about hip-hop and Adidas and designer jeans. We were riding around in Samurai Suzukis and Jeeps with the top off, sound system in the back. Our poetry was LL Cool J, MC Lyte, and Run DMC. But, here, I became aware of influences from all over—the Caribbean, the West Coast, the South.

Before I ever got to Oakwood, though, my father who raised me urged me toward a kind of awareness that I didn't know I needed. When I was twelve, I brought home a school photo of the girl I liked. Her name was Sarah. She was pretty and smart, and she liked me back—always important. I showed the photo to my mom. My dad only glanced at it. The thing was that Sarah was white. On the surface, I didn't know her whiteness was a problem, but in the back of my mind, I had a feeling that maybe it might be.

The next day, when my dad got home from his shift at GM, he handed me a paperback copy of *The Autobiography of Malcolm X*. The cover had my man in his horn-rimmed glasses, looking sharp in his suit and tie. It was small enough to fit into my back pocket, so I carried it around with me. I took it downstairs to the basement where I had a weight set. Every day after school, I would lift and take a break, sitting on the edge of the bench, chipping away at Malcolm's story—his father's murder by the KKK, his mother's struggle with mental illness, getting separated from his siblings. It was the first time I had ever heard of the Ku Klux Klan, and the idea that you could be killed for the color of your skin. I was shocked that something like that could even exist in America. I was so sheltered, living a certain version of the American dream, that it hit hard.

You have to remember, when I was reading Malcolm, it felt close. He'd spent time in Detroit, lived in Lansing as a young man, and had been assassinated in New York only seventeen years before. Even though I wasn't alive when he was around, people in Detroit talked about him like it was yesterday. They didn't necessarily feel his belief in Islam—most everybody we knew was Christian—but Malcolm represented a moment when Black Americans were reclaiming their power and becoming aware of the beauty of our history. Around that time, I also started watching *Roots*, which Alex Haley, Malcolm X's ghostwriter, wrote, too.

When you find your way, you find a way to make it happen.

I carried the *Autobiography* to school in my backpack like a totem. It made me feel like I was getting to know my people, and it brought me into a more adult conversation with my family. My mother was a reader, which I admired. My uncle Ben, whom we called Uncle Hebrew, was a music-head and knew everything about Black history. He encouraged me to talk about what I was learning. I talked to the OGs in the neighborhood about it, and my uncle David, who was heavy into Black thought, introduced me to magazines like *Jet* and *Ebony*. He taught me about Kareem Abdul-Jabbar, Jesse Jackson, and Wilt Chamberlain. And we talked about Malcolm, too. I was fixated on this story of a man who transformed his entire life and created a vision for his people through what seemed like sheer will. This was what purpose looked like. This is what was possible if you could find a path and then dedicate your entire life to walking on it.

When I got to the part in the *Autobiography* about Malcolm getting into a relationship with a white woman, I stopped reading. Back then, I don't think I could articulate why, but I must have felt in my heart what my father's message was. We lived in a neighborhood where all the men were married to Black women, where the concept of self-love meant loving a woman who looked like you. Back then we just said love; today people call it Black love. Reading the *Autobiography* was the first time I understood that loving someone outside of your own race could be dangerous.

When I ask my mom about this moment, she doesn't remember the photo. She says she wouldn't have thought about it that way. Her father was biracial and her grandfather was white, so it wouldn't have occurred to her to have warned me off in the same way. But she also tells me about her light-skinned cousin who left for the military early to stay out of trouble with white women. She talks about her stepfather's family who favored her darker-skinned siblings. She remembers hearing about her father having to pass as Cuban or Italian just so he could get a job when he was living in Chicago and Indiana. My father who raised me had a different perspective. He went to college in Texas and traveled the country playing college basketball. There were places he wasn't allowed to stay. Sometimes he and his teammates had to sleep on the bus because no hotel would welcome them. There were communities where he was refused entrance. And he knew that growing up as a Black boy in America could be dangerous.

After reading Malcolm X, I stayed friends with Sarah, but I couldn't see it the same way I did before. And maybe her parents were at home trying to persuade her I wasn't a fit for her either. I'll never know.

Today, I see what my father was doing in giving me that book. What happened in my freshman year of Oakwood was what he wanted to happen for me at the age of twelve or thirteen. He wanted me to grow up and see what the world was like, to see what I could be, and to move through life with more intention. When I got to Oakwood, it just clicked. Maybe it's because I was with 1,800 other students who were interested in the same things—my peers rather than my parents—and we were embracing it all together. But as soon as it locked into place, I felt that I knew something about myself. I felt that I had a new connection to my superpower. And that feeling filled me with more purpose and direction than I'd ever known before.

My self-esteem flourished in this time. Academically, I wasn't the most impressive student, and at Bell Tower I was more like Dennis Rodman—the support guy—than Michael Jordan, but I was finding out who I was and I excelled at bringing people together. When I started to feel that confidence rise up in me, it's funny, but I also started to treat myself differently. I started talking to myself differently. Here I was, a broken kid from Detroit, academically bereft, without much direction. And when people started listening to me, captivated by my voice, I felt like I was moving toward something bigger than just me. Most kids didn't like going to chapel to worship—they'd be ready to get out as soon as we said Amen—but at the Bell Tower, people wanted to be there, and they wanted to listen to us and to me. With my newfound confidence, I started thinking differently. I started participating in life.

Power Becomes Purpose When You Have a Plan

Purpose is nothing without structure and standards. You could discover your superpower and have a why, but if you don't impose structure and standards on your life, your purpose is without a path. Power does not become purpose without a schedule and a plan. Even if you aren't clear on what the end goal is—I promise you, I didn't think I was headed toward becoming a famous motivational speaker—you have to honor your purpose by giving it boundaries. You have to practice it. You have to organize your time around it. You have to nurture and study it. You have to get to know how to move through your purpose with intention.

Bell Tower gave me structure. I had a place to be. I had a direction to go in. Standing up and speaking three times a week and feeling people listening to me got me wondering what else I might be able to do with my life. My superpower was not only activated, but I was directing it in a way that felt intentional. I was figuring out how to turn it on, where and when to turn it on, when to rest it, and feeling more confident in the very fact that it existed. Whereas before, in school, I was bouncing off the walls, talking and chopping it up and joking without any sort of real direction or method, now I was focusing my efforts in one intense burst of energy. And, in focusing, I got to know myself better.

I started to understand my appeal and my particular strengths in

113

speaking. Where Irv was doing a lot of theoretical stuff, breaking down a text in Hebrew or Greek, and Tres was all about the spirituality, my swag has always been simplicity. Even back then, my work was about getting in touch with yourself, thinking about how you communicate with your parents and your peers, how to adjust your life to enjoy it, and embracing failure and challenges alongside the victories. My speaking style has always been about the passion behind the message.

You are the director and screenwriter of your life.

I would come up with a pared-down one-liner to get people to understand the point. For instance: "Break the cycle, I dare you." This one little line encompassed an entire message about breaking the generational cycle of poverty, of getting educated, of creating a legacy. This one-line challenge made the message memorable. People have always told me that there's something about the quality of my voice that moves

them, that makes them want to run through walls. I think it's also because I know myself and I can talk about my experiences with raw hon-
esty. I've never been afraid to tell anybody about my struggles. Talking
about my struggles helps people see their way through their own struggles. Struggling is part of finding yourself. Struggling is all part of finding
your purpose. But you never have to struggle alone.

I found purpose in being part of a collective endeavor. A big part of
what we talked about was doing our part in the struggle together. Educating ourselves. Becoming W. E. B. Du Bois's Talented Tenth—the
classically educated individual who would represent our community to
the world. We talked about becoming contributors, taking up our right-
ful places with excellence. We studied speaking styles together, sitting
around and listening to speeches by Malcolm X and Desmond Tutu. We
listened to James Brown's "Black and Proud," Marvin Gaye's "What's
Going On," and Curtis Mayfield. We did sit-ins for Nelson Mandela's
freedom and visited Atlanta to see the Martin Luther King Jr. museum,
where Coretta Scott King showed up unannounced and prayed with us.
We visited the 16th Street Baptist Church in Birmingham, where those
four little girls had been killed by a bomb. We talked about the greatest
Black thinkers in America and if we had a place among them. Being part
of something bigger than myself gave me focus and energy.

Eventually, Bell Tower became legend, and everybody knew us
around campus. Oakwood's professors started to take an interest in us.
When prospective students came around, the administration would give
us a lighting system and artists would come out to show their work. Bell
Tower became part of the appeal of coming to Oakwood. It distinguished
us from other places. Eventually, our following expanded beyond campus
and we were given the opportunity to travel around the South, speaking

at revivals and churches for days at a time. We went to Georgia and Bermuda and all over Alabama. I started to receive invitations to go out and speak on my own when Irv and Tres had other stuff going on.

Of course, in my junior year I started teaching the GED course, later became a substitute teacher, and eventually dropped out of college, but as long as I was in Huntsville, I was doing the Bell, 1989 to 1998. And even though I wasn't working toward my degree, I was there studying for something else. I was participating in the world, meeting people who supported me, and getting to know myself. I didn't have a career to speak of—I was working at Olive Garden to pay the bills—but, even so, I was discovering my purpose.

A purpose doesn't always correlate to your career. Of course, your purpose can become your career, but a purpose is more about using your gifts and moving in the awareness of them. Using your gifts often manifests in the form of what I like to call "the intangibles." Intangibles are the things you do to use and grow your gifts without expecting anything in return. For instance, Bell Tower wasn't about making money or gaining notoriety. It was about spreading a message and finding connection. For me, teaching has never been about building a career or flexing my ego. It's about helping people identify and embrace their own power and purpose and why. Even today, when a major part of my career and income depends on motivational speaking, I still give away my work. My series, *Thank God It's Monday*, or *TGIM*, has always been free. My podcast, my videos, my social media—it's all about giving of my gifts. As much as I can, when I travel to speak or work with a team, I stop at the schools in the local community. I go to the juvenile detention center. I stop at the Boys & Girls Clubs. These intangibles are like exercising or conditioning. They keep you walking toward your purpose. They keep you focused. And they build your relationship with the world around you. Walking in your purpose is equally about building your gifts and giving them away to people who need them. And when you give your gifts away, the world blesses you in return.

Your Why Is What Drives Purpose

Over time, purpose shifts and deepens. When you get to know your superpower more intimately, it changes how you move through your purpose. When your why becomes better defined and more layered, your purpose, too, becomes clearer and more complex. In my case, purpose was made clearer with crisis.

By 2012, Dede and I were killing it. We were settled in Michigan. She had a great job at the Ingham County Health Department in Lansing. I was all over the country, speaking and building my company. Our kids were grown—Jalin had just graduated from high school and Jayda was in her sophomore year. We had enough money to feel comfortable. We had vacation time. My business with CJ was booming. Life was good.

But one day Dede called me on her way home from work. I'll never forget the sound of her voice. She was confused and a little scared. She said she was in her car, and had taken her usual route home from the hospital, which was almost a straight shot from door to door. She'd done it every day for the last five years. But somewhere along the way she'd taken a wrong turn and she had no idea where she was or how she'd gotten there. Around the same time Dede's legs had started aching, too, which she'd attributed to all the work involved in organizing Jalin's graduation party, but when the celebration had died down, the aching wouldn't go away. The second time she got lost on her way home, we went to the doctor. Immediately, they did an MRI, and the radiologist, who was a family friend, called us to tell us what she'd seen. There were lesions on Dede's brain. A few days later, the doctor talked to us about the diagnosis. Dede had multiple sclerosis. It felt like being at a funeral. The person I had dreamed of life with at fifteen, sixteen years old, the person I had taken a vow of forever with was sick, and I had no control over it. My why was in trouble.

When your why is in danger, you will do everything you can to protect it. You start living not just with purpose, but with passion. And the person who lives with passion is dangerous. They have a no-surrender mind-set. They will stop at nothing to make the dream a reality.

When Dede was diagnosed with MS, I was in a state of shock. My brain struggled to square how this was possible. We didn't drink, we didn't smoke, we exercised, we ate well. Dede was in good shape, and she had never had issues with chronic illness in her life. My father who raised me has MS and was diagnosed when he was in his thirties, but I wasn't at the crib when he and my mom started going through that, so I had no idea what it meant. Everybody's experience with the disease is different. And, for Dede and me, it was life-altering.

Multiple sclerosis is an autoimmune disease that causes your immune system to attack your nervous system, which results in a whole range of symptoms: vision loss, numb hands and feet, fatigue, slurred speech. The doctors laid out the potential challenges: Dede might lose mobility, and her ability to talk or swallow or even see. The doctor also spelled out the potential paths for treatment: She could try a holistic diet to see how her body responded and/or start taking medication that would slow or stop the growth of lesions on her brain. We decided to try both.

In the beginning, Dede was optimistic, but when the doctor told her she had to stop working she was devastated. Dede comes from a family of strong women. Her mother was never married and was one of fifteen children whose own mother raised them alone after her husband left. They all worked and they all took care of themselves and they were all very proud of their self-made lives. Dede embodies the meaning of the term *independent woman*. I like to joke around with her that she's actually an alpha male. She doesn't want to rely on anyone for anything. Even when she was going off to college and her mom offered to buy her a car, Dede wouldn't take it. She worked for it and paid for it herself.

When you have MS, you have to avoid stress as much as possible, and Dede's career as a nurse was stressful. She loved it, though, and she tried to keep doing it for a while, but it became clear pretty quickly that maintaining her career was untenable. Retiring was the beginning of the end of the old Dede. She realized that she had to look to me for all her support, and would have to trust that I could take care of her physically, financially, and emotionally. Of course, we'd been building a life together for almost thirty years, but this was a new level of needing each other.

When Dede started taking her medication, things got real. Every day, she had to put a needle somewhere in her body. Monday it was her left arm. Tuesday it was her right arm. Wednesday it was her left leg. Thursday it was her right leg. Friday it was her stomach. And Saturday she'd start all over again. The needles left bruises on her body, so she started wearing pants and long sleeves, even in the summer. In the first eight months, there were times where all she could do was sleep and eat, and she needed to be nursed like a baby.

Sometimes Dede would talk to me about her guilt—about what awful timing her diagnosis was, and how bad she felt for keeping me at home. My career was blowing up. The "Secret to Success" video was out there, and that joker had millions of views already. But I didn't think of it that way. What was beautiful about this moment was the reaffirmation of my why. I knew it was my opportunity to show up for Dede, the strongest person that I'd ever known. It was my chance to be with her in sickness, to give her everything I had in my own health. For years, I had been walking in my purpose, giving 100, but when Dede got sick, I got fully in my gifts and fully in my purpose. I had to give more.

Success is not a destination, it's a journey.

Before chronic illness became part of my family's life, I didn't have to go 120. Together, Dede and I made a full team, but when she couldn't work anymore, I started doing double duty. I cooked, cleaned, and got Jayda to all her activities—all while traveling and speaking to keep us financially stable. But, eventually, I realized that if I were going to balance it all, I had to work smarter. I couldn't be leaving on the weekends when Dede was in her most vulnerable state. I couldn't be gone for days at a time on the road. I thought I was grinding when I was getting up at 3 a.m., being out traveling 24/7, but it turns out that I was still holding a little bit of something back. I had awareness of my gifts, and I was on a path, but it wasn't until Dede got sick that I began truly living in my full purpose.

When everything went down with Dede, I discovered that I had more to give. And this is the truth. We always have more. We evolve. We grow stronger. We gain the ability to do more and to give more. You can always go further and deeper than you know. Sometimes we get complacent. We let comfort and stability and predictability get in the way. These things aren't bad, but they do impede progress. They pull your foot off the gas and they make you forget that life is a journey, rather than a destination.

Growing up in Detroit, my mom had a garden out back. She used to go buy manure, put it all over the plots, and watch it grow. She was paying top dollar for premium crap. Crap is what makes things grow. To produce vegetables, you need water, light, and crap. That's the formula. It's the same in our lives. The stuff that nourishes us is sometimes awful. The awful stuff can push us to go to the next level, to fight more fiercely for our why, to embody purpose with the fullness and clarity we might not have otherwise. These moments of struggle and difficulty can be used to your advantage. They can be harnessed to push you further than you'd ever go alone. The hardest moments in your life are the ones that make you stronger.

The Work

1. What do you love doing? What about the doing is pleasurable or satisfying? How does it affect other people? What do you love doing that affects the people around you positively? When you see this effect, how does it make you feel?

2. What change would you like to see in the world? What do you do in your life that would help bring about this change? What could you be doing in your own way to effect this change? Is this part of your career path or something outside of it? Do you want it to be part of your career or to keep it separate?

3. Do you have structure around the things you love to do—a schedule, a group you work with, etc.? When was the last time you made time to do what you love? Do you have a plan for doing more of it?

Challenge: Remind yourself of your gifts. Remind yourself of your superpower. Make a list of the things that you do with your gifts or superpower every day. What are the results of these gifts? Who do they touch? Who do they help? Who else enjoys them? Imagine how the results of these gifts might look if you amplified them to reach your group of friends, your family, your coworkers. Now imagine how the results of these gifts might look if extended to your community. How does that manifest concretely? What do you need to do to begin using your gifts in a way that touches everyone around you? Now remember your why. How can you use your gifts to meet up with your why?

CHAPTER

Put Yourself in Miracle Territory

YOU CAN ATTRACT YOUR OWN MIRACLES.

Most people think miracles are a phenomenon of nature or some sort of supernatural wonder. But I can tell you, miracles are born of intention. The biggest opportunities of my life came about because I put myself in the way of them. When I began walking in my purpose with real intention, the world responded and gave me miracles big and small. There's a ripple effect when you exercise your gifts. The ripples get bigger and bigger until they become waves. These waves—and even the ripples—are miracles.

I'll give you an example. For years, I worked for free, giving my gifts away, speaking at Oakwood, speaking at schools, speaking in the community around Huntsville. As Bell Tower blew up, I got invited to do individual gigs all over. I began traveling and going to conferences. I got connected with the education system and academia. When I began working in schools, the people who ran them recognized that I had a way with kids who needed education the most. At some point, I was asked to speak in Atlanta for Kenny Anderson, a psychology professor at Oakwood. Professor Anderson worked with a conference hosted by San Diego State in Atlanta that was all about helping Black kids stay in school and get through their education at predominantly white institutions. I presented for ten or fifteen minutes, explained my method of teaching the GED, and gave some of my students the opportunity to share their experiences.

Through that event, I got invited to Louisville for the Black Family Conference. Someone there saw me speak, and invited me to the Black Man Think Tank in Cincinnati. This is how opportunities work—one

125

leads to another. And in Cincinnati, I got an opportunity that would change everything. What I didn't realize until later was that all the speakers for the Black Man Think Tank were set. I wasn't supposed to even be on the speaking lineup, but I'd been so effective in my previous appearances, that I was given the honor of introducing Dr. Na'im Akbar, the famous African American psychologist, for his own talk.

This was a big deal for me. Dr. Akbar changed my way of thinking when I first read his book, *Visions for Black Men*. Although a lot of his language and theory was too advanced for me to understand at the time, I latched on to his ideas about how African American males develop. In our community, the stages of childhood, adolescence, and adulthood are not always super defined, and, as a result, some kids are at risk of growing up too quickly in some aspects while not maturing in others. When I read *Visions*, it helped me understand what it means to go from male to manhood. It was what my father who raised me was trying to get me to understand when he gave me *The Autobiography of Malcolm X* all those years ago.

When I got the chance to introduce Dr. Akbar, it was a turning point—and a small miracle. I was opening for a man of ideas, a man who developed theories that influenced me and my generation. By standing on a stage to introduce him, I was suddenly associated with a whole new part of my field. My purpose felt expanded.

The conference for the Black Man Think Tank took place in an old-fashioned indoor theater with burgundy carpets, velvet curtains held back with big tasseled ropes, and a second floor that overlooked the regal stage. While I was waiting in the wings, I peeked out and saw a whole different audience than I usually spoke to. I was used to getting up in front of middle school kids, high school kids, college kids. But this was an audience of my peers. I was twenty-four, twenty-five years old and I was in a room with myself and my brothers. This was a space of academics and distinguished people, too—my uncles, my fathers, my elders. I knew the codes, the cues, the language, but to say I was nervous would be an understatement.

When I stand up in front of an audience I think about where I am, who I'm speaking to, and what they're there for. In this case, I was in the Midwest, so I had home court advantage. In 'Bama, I talk more slowly because the pace is slower and more laid-back. But there, I could talk at my regular speed. I also knew I was the opening act. When you're at a show to see Beyoncé, you want to see Beyoncé. You're just waiting for the opener to get offstage. So I knew I had to grab people's attention quickly and keep my energy steady. I knew I had to pace myself, but also keep it quick.

Just offstage, there was a full-length mirror, and I stood in front of it, practicing and practicing, until finally I heard my name called. I came on and did my thing. I talked about where I was in my life—a high school dropout who went to college, a college dropout who made it to this stage somehow, who had been affected by Dr. Akbar's understanding of my life on a theoretical level. To close it out, I broke down Dr. Akbar's analogy of a caterpillar retreating into a cocoon to emerge as a butterfly. I ended it all in a crescendo about showing the world how I was going to fly, fly, fly, and, by the end, the whole audience was feeling me. They were on their feet, cheering and clapping, and when I left the stage I felt what Olympic swimmer Michael Phelps must have felt after preparing his entire life to swim that first 100-meter butterfly in front of the entire world. You get a few seconds, a few minutes to really embody your true purpose, and then it's over and you just know you've killed it.

At the end, everybody came up to me. "Young man, what's your name? Where you from? You did a phenomenal job. Take my card." People gave me their cards—people from Ohio University, Kent State, Morehouse, Howard, Tuskegee, University of Kentucky—cats from all over. That day, I got pulled aside by two men who would change my life. Murray Edwards and Rodney Patterson introduced themselves and told me they wanted me to come to Michigan State University.

Miracles Are the Product of Intent

Meeting Murray Edwards and Rodney Patterson was a miracle. It changed my whole life trajectory. On the surface, this may not seem like a miracle—just a chance encounter of right place, right time. But I see it is as a phenomenon in its own right. Miracles happen when you put yourself in the way of them. And performing to the best of your abilities gets you into that territory. Up until that point, I had been grinding and grinding. Finally, when I intersected with the moment I'd been waiting for, I was ready for it.

Murray and Rodney invited me to come talk to the students in their program, the Black Male Initiative (BMI), which targeted young Black men to give them the support they needed to succeed in the predominantly white institution of Michigan State. This was everything I was already about. I was from Michigan. I was already in the game of helping young people of color understand the language of education. I was making my own way in the world, understanding the systems around me and how to navigate them. There was nothing more on-brand for me.

That year, I started regularly traveling to Michigan from Huntsville to speak to the kids in BMI. I would do my thing, give them the kick start they needed during midterms or finals. I worked with a program that brought freshman kids from the inner city to spend a week on campus to get them acclimated before everyone else got there. I'd show up whenever Murray and Rodney needed someone who could get on the kids' level, see them for who they were, and get them pumped. And then I'd head back home.

Every time I went to Michigan, I would stay a little bit longer. I'd go see my mom in Detroit, and then drive the hour and a half to East Lansing. It felt familiar, but at the same time, it made me feel alive. A few years into this routine, Murray and Rodney told me I needed to come finish my degree. I thought about it all the time. I was just shy of getting my bachelor's at Oakwood, and I knew I had to finish it to keep moving forward. It was weird, me teaching kids about getting a degree without having one myself. Somehow, I was taking students to the next level without a real plan or strategy for myself. It was clear that I had to do something to change that—to practice what I was preaching. Murray and Rodney were recruiting me like an athlete—offering me a fellowship and a job as an academic adviser—and it all felt like a natural progression.

When I talked to my father who raised me about leaving Alabama to finish my degree at MSU, he advised me to stay at Oakwood. Most of my credits likely wouldn't have transferred, so I'd have to start from scratch, and he knew I had a habit of not following through on my education. So, I put it in my mind that I would feel more accomplished if I just did what I'd set out to do years before. In the end, it took me twelve years to get a four-year degree, but when I got that cap and gown, and walked up for my diploma, I knew I was moving toward something so much bigger. When I finally finished in 2003, I was ready to leave Oakwood.

Lansing had gotten buzzy, starting in 1998 when Coach Tom Izzo arrived and Spartan basketball was on fire. There was something magnetic about the place that I couldn't get out of my head. In Huntsville, I'd gone as far as I could go—people were telling me I should run for mayor. I didn't have a real plan, but I felt like Michigan was my place. To me, Michigan was miracle territory.

Dede, however, did not agree. In Dede's mind, I was being impulsive. I was regressing into that homeless dreamer she'd met when she was fifteen years old. This was Mr. Optimistic talking to Ms. Realistic about opportunities and miracles without any promise of stability. She couldn't understand how I could want to uproot our entire lives for something that wasn't a sure bet. I had an invitation from Michigan State for a fellowship to MSU and a potential job as an academic adviser, but I hadn't signed any papers. Nothing was official. We didn't know what life in East Lansing would look like. We'd worked so hard to establish our careers and our relationships in Huntsville that to leave it all behind seemed irresponsible. Dede and I had been dreaming of this life together since we were teenagers, and the way she saw it, I was coming in and razing it all to the ground. This was biggest moment of strife we'd ever had in our relationship.

Dede wanted me to go spend time in East Lansing for a few months to check things out, scout the lay of the land if you will, and report back. But I knew I couldn't leave my family behind. It wouldn't be the same, and I felt like I needed her full support to make everything work. I told her I needed her and the kids, that I needed to see them every day to know what life could be like fully in this choice.

I had put a lot of thought into it, and all my experiences and intuition told me that this was the right move. Sure, there was risk involved, but it was a calculated risk. I had connections. I had people rooting for me. I had evidence that I was successful and could transfer that success to another place. But for Dede, it was still scary. There was no guarantee it would work out.

To get to that next level, you gotta learn to get comfortable being uncomfortable.

This is what putting yourself in miracle territory can feel like. It can feel risky or impulsive. It can feel lonely. In my mind, I thought this should be the most exciting time of my life, but, in reality, taking risks to get to the next level can be painful and difficult. It's like having a child. It's a beautiful thing, giving birth, but it comes with pain and risk, too. When you want to do great things and forge new paths, you must brace yourself for the efforts that it takes to be great and to carve out new territory. It might cause friction in your relationships with family, friends, or your business partner. But if you know it's the right move, you know. The key is to slow down and communicate your feelings and plans to the people around you. Tell them what you're going after, why it's important to you, and what you're going to do to make it real. Miracles are beautiful things, but they also require work and trust and mutual cooperation. Miracles, at some level, are always logical.

In the case of moving to MSU, everything I'd done was pointing to this moment. All the tangible and intangible things I'd been working on—taking the GED, getting to Oakwood, starting Bell Tower, teaching the GED, becoming a teacher—this harnessing of my superpower and walking in my purpose was putting me in the position to attract opportunities. And being in the position to attract opportunities is putting yourself in miracle territory.

Here's the thing about miracles: They don't just happen. There is intentionality around them. Nobody just calls you and says, "Here's the job you've always been dreaming of" or "Hey, your long-lost uncle left you a million bucks in his will." Miracles aren't the supernatural, science-defying events we imagine them to be. The finer details of how they happen are often a matter of timing and lighting, but miracles and their results are things we wish for. They're things we set intentions around. In so many terms, I tried to explain to Dede that this was the moment we'd been waiting for. And I can't say she was fully onboard. Or even onboard at all. But somehow she agreed to move.

In 2003, we packed up our cars with Jayda and Jalin and as many clothes as we could carry, hitched Dede's Mercury Tracer-Trio to my Suburban, and drove north. We left behind an entire house full of things. We didn't have a renter or a buyer or an alarm system, and we didn't have a solid plan. Dede quit a job she loved. Jayda was headed to kindergarten and Jalin was going into third grade, and we had no idea where we would enroll them when we arrived. We had no idea where we were going to live. Dede was pissed. She didn't talk to me for the entire trip. For the almost 700 miles from Huntsville to East Lansing, we drove in complete silence.

When we finally arrived, the university put us up in their hotel on campus. For a month, we lived in an outdated room with dark green carpet, two double beds, big heavy Queen Anne furniture, and a desk where we'd make peanut butter and jelly sandwiches every day. Jayda and Jalin had no yard to play in, so they ran around the hallways when they weren't at school. Nobody had any privacy, and we lived half out of our cars because there was no place to put anything. We shuttled back and forth to the parking garage to pick out an outfit or a pair of shoes. Every day, we had vouchers to eat in the dining room downstairs, but it wasn't great cooking. We helped the kids with their homework, spread out across the floor every night. And, of course, Dede still wouldn't talk to me.

Eventually, we got campus housing in an apartment complex near the university. It was bigger, but everything was old and falling apart. The kitchen linoleum was yellow, the appliances were outdated, and, on the weekends, it was a constant party up and down the hallways. I remember watching kids carry in beer kegs and listening to their music through the walls from Friday to Sunday, all night long. For months, Dede was not the same. I think she felt that I had betrayed our shared dream—that I'd traded it in for something abstract and unstable.

But even in the darker days I felt a newness. I felt hope. I knew I couldn't spread my wings at a four-year college. I perceived a ceiling in Huntsville, and it made me feel stifled—like I was a plant outgrowing a pot, and my roots were getting ready to break through my container. I knew I needed to be someplace different to get to the next level. I also

133

knew that I wanted our kids to experience what it was like to live near a world-class campus like Michigan State. All those talented people—athletes, academics, intellectuals from all over the world. Even though I didn't know exactly what was coming next, I knew I was in the right place.

Eventually, Dede had a serious emotional experience. She went to God and asked him for what she needed. I think in some ways, she surrendered and in surrendering found exactly what she was looking for. Soon after, she landed a great job as a nurse for the county, first with women's health and then working with women dealing with breast and cervical cancer. She was near her mom and family in Detroit and could go back and forth to see them on the weekends. She started going to a local church and building a community again.

And the move worked out. In the years to come, I got my master's and PhD at MSU and my whole life—our whole lives—changed. The move became the launchpad for everything else. The move brought about all the miracles to come.

Receiving Miracles Is Not a Passive Act

Putting yourself in miracle territory is when you actively use your gifts and in doing so create new possibilities for yourself. Miracle territory is the place where you find possibilities opening up and the world ready to receive your purpose.

Actively using your gifts is walking in your purpose. And using your gifts doesn't always mean you will benefit financially or that you should expect something in return. When you wake up every day walking in your purpose, rather than looking for a paycheck, you are creating intangible value. Intangible value is what underpins and gives shape to your tangible value. Intangible value has the ability to attract miracles.

The difference between those who succeed and those who fail: not taking advantage of opportunities.

In my life, this has been true almost 100 percent of the time. For example, I have always attended conferences to listen to other people speak. I started attending them not to be the headline speaker, but to connect with organizations that were doing work I felt aligned with my own beliefs and values. I was never there to run the joint. When I started showing up to events, I was there to organize. I was there to get things done and help other people get their thing done. I was there to set up rooms, pick people up from the airport, pass out lunch to the attendees. I was there to clean and vacuum when everybody else had gone home.

Attending conferences and events was about learning for me, and about being of service. Service is a perfect example of building intangible value. Taking out trash and setting up rooms wasn't making me money. It wasn't a skill I could put on a résumé or one that would get me further in my education. But it was getting me into the rooms where things were happening, where people were connecting, and opportunities were available. When you build your intangible value, you put yourself in a space to attract opportunity. If you're an asset to the people around you, you begin to attract opportunity. And opportunities are miracles in their own right.

Receiving miracles is not a passive act. It's anything but.

Everybody wants to be great. Everybody wants to experience what they consider to be the American dream. The funny thing is that a lot of people think they need some stroke of luck to achieve greatness. They think they need to win the lottery or hit it big in Vegas to get to that place of financial or emotional security. And, sure, the lottery can be miracle territory. Vegas can be miracle territory. But it's miracle territory you don't have much control over. Winning the lottery or hitting it big at a slot machine is a one-in-a-million chance. Working on your gifts and receiving opportunities is highly doable.

Think about this: People get aggressive about playing the lottery, lining up every day to grab a ticket. People are willing to sit around for hours and gamble on their computers. They get aggressive about going to Vegas, planning the trip, spending money at the slots or by the tables. But when it comes to their own abilities, they're passive. Instead of using their earnings to invest in their education or learn more about their gifts, they take a back seat and expect things to come to them.

I didn't just sit around and wait for people to come ask me to speak at their events. I wasn't necessarily always planning to become the main event I am today, but I knew if I wanted to have any influence, I had to work my way to the top. I had to show up and try. I had to pave the path to my own miracle. Using your gifts every single day, even when it doesn't totally make sense, is putting yourself in miracle territory. This is how I met my business partner CJ.

When I first started going to MSU, I worked with a football coach at Sexton, a working-class middle school in East Lansing. One day in 2005, Coach Daniel Bogan invited me over to the school to talk to some kids for a program he was running, but I had a conflicting gig at MSU so I had to decline. On the day of the gig, MSU canceled, so I went over to Sexton to see if they still needed me. I could have gone home and taken the rest of the day off, but, like working out or praying, I have made it a committed practice to exercise my gifts every day, so I just showed up to see what I could help with. Coach Bogan had already filled up the day's roster and didn't have a slot for me to speak. But he told me to hang tight and sat me at a table with some other people while he went to see what he could rearrange.

I got to talking to a man named Carlas Quinney Sr. He was in his late forties and heavily involved in football programs around the city. His own boys had played football, and he just liked being in the mix of coaching and player development. Through our conversation, I told him I was teaching at MSU, doing academic advising, and working on the Black Male Initiative. His eyes lit up, and then he looked at me very seriously and told me I needed to meet his son, who was a junior on campus. He explained that his son was killing the game as an academic adviser and mentor, and it was crazy that we hadn't met yet. So I gave him my card and told Carlas to send him on over to my office.

That was a Friday. As CJ tells it, his dad called him as soon as he got home and told him he needed to come speak with me first thing on Monday. CJ told him he would. On Saturday morning, his dad called him again to remind him. CJ agreed again that he would. On Sunday his dad called and said the same thing. Monday morning, too. CJ was a little bit weirded out by how adamant his dad was about this—C is the kind of person who has a deep sense of internal motivation and doesn't need anybody to push him to get involved or meet new people. He would have come and seen me without his dad's encouragement, but it was Carlas Sr.'s encouragement that I think drove home the potential for our connection.

When he showed up to my office on Monday morning, CJ was CJ. Never lacking for confidence, he was eager to tell me about the awards and accolades he'd already received. He had just been working with the mayor and governor, and had been honored as mentor of the year at MSU. We sat down and I showed him a video of a speech I'd just done in Omaha, Nebraska, which impressed him. Neither of us knew it in those first moments, but we'd become business partners and best friends for life. Since that day, CJ and I have never been apart. This was another miracle of opportunity.

I didn't have to go to see Coach Bogan after my gig at MSU was canceled. I could have gone home and put my feet up, but as somebody who is committed to walking in my purpose, I was serious about using my superpower every single day. The simple choice to do so put me in the position to receive the connection with the person who eventually took me to the next level. CJ is the person who has been able to translate my work and my gifts into a business. Without him, I know I wouldn't be where I am today. It's possible CJ and I would have met somewhere else on campus some other day. It's possible we might have ended up at another event together somewhere down the road and exchanged contact information. But I came to him through his father, who validated me and advocated for me. It was a miracle that we connected in the way we did.

Miracles Can Appear in the Most Obvious Places

CJ and I started a program at Michigan State called the Advantage. We named it that because we were working in a predominantly white institution that was predominantly concerned with the needs of the 93 percent of students who were white. This automatically gave those students certain advantages. What our program was built to do was to prepare and counsel those kids whom the academic system doesn't necessarily focus on. Our program would give them the advantage they were lacking.

The Advantage was an outgrowth of BMI. CJ and I had a feeling we could build something new and different, something that we could take to other schools and expand to new audiences beyond MSU. Eventually, this dream became a reality. Every Monday we would get all our kids in a room somewhere on campus, and I'd stand up to speak and motivate them for the week to come. And at some point, the Advantage started attracting demographics beyond the kids we'd set it up for. We even had people traveling from outside the school to see what we had going on. Young, old, Black, white—the Advantage was serving everybody who needed it.

The Advantage opened us up to new miracle territory: the internet.

If you know me, you know about the "Secret to Success" video. Putting

that joker on YouTube was putting ourselves in the greatest miracle territory we could have imagined. If you already know about the guru story,
you know. But you might not know how it went down.

It happened in a classroom at Michigan State. It was October 2006.
I'd been living in Lansing for about three years. We'd started the Advantage the year before. I was thirty-six, working on my PhD, and just grinding. I had been speaking for years. Motivational speaking wasn't
necessarily my bread and butter, as it is today, but I already knew it was
my spiritual calling, and I was getting known for it around the MSU
campus, too. I treated speaking the way an athlete treats practice: It's
about repetition. It's about muscle memory. Doing something over and
over and over again to get better and better. Even back then, I was speaking nearly every day to some group somewhere. Every time I speak, it's
special. It's new. It's urgent. It's never the same. That day was no different. I was doing what I do best. But it was also just another day in the life
of ET.

The group of kids I was speaking to in that classroom that particular
day were part of the Advantage program. It was just before midterms.
Many of them were in a tenuous position. If they didn't get their acts
together and ace their tests, they were going to get kicked out of school
and sent home. And for many of those kids, to go home would be devastating. Getting to MSU was a dream that seemed impossible in the first
place. To forfeit that dream would mean going back to the projects or a
hometown where opportunity is sparse and advanced education is nonexistent. The results of their upcoming midterms would be a defining
moment—one that would literally determine their future. I knew when
I walked into that classroom that my message had to be urgent. To me, it
felt like life or death.

The story I told went something like this: A man who wants to get ahead in business goes to a guru and says to him, "People say you know the secret to success. What's the secret, guru?"

The guru says, "If you want to learn the secret, meet me down by the beach early tomorrow morning."

So, the next morning the man shows up to the beach in a suit to meet the guru. The guru tells the man to follow him out into the water. The man looks at the guru like he's crazy, but he does it anyway. When the water is chest-high, the guru shoves the man's head down and holds him under until he's struggling and flailing his arms. Eventually, the guru lets the man surface. When he finally catches his breath, the guru asks the man: "When you were underneath the water, what did you want more than anything?"

The man answers him: "To breathe."

The guru nods and says, "Now you know the secret. When you want to succeed as bad as you want to breathe, you will be successful."

There was more to the talk, of course, but this was the part that people know the best. It's the part people play over and over again. Compared to other things I've done, the "Secret to Success" video might not look like much. It's kind of grainy, and I'm wearing a button-down shirt I'd never wear today. But it's me, all right. And it's my voice. And it's the tipping point of my career. I didn't know it, of course. I had no idea that this little video would be the fuel that got me to the next level. I had no idea I would walk through airports and down streets, and people would stop me and say, "I know you—you're the guru guy." I didn't know people would start wearing T-shirts with my face or my quotes on them. All I knew in that moment was that I wanted these kids to listen and feel in their bones what I had to tell them. This is how I always feel when I

141

stand up and talk to a group of kids who are on the precipice of their future.

Only when you want to succeed as bad as you want to breathe will you be successful.

The only difference between that day and any other day was that there was a camera in that room and there was a mic on my collar. A guy I knew from the school, named Kenneth Nelson, asked if he could record me giving one of my talks. And I thought, *Why not?* Being willing to try something new puts you in miracle territory, too.

Here's the thing: I'd been doing those talks. I'd been counseling those kids. Before that day, I'd had a twelve-year speaking career. Every week, I'd be in juvenile detention centers with boys whose lives were on a downward spiral that couldn't be stopped, kids whose parents had been killed, or who'd watched their friends die in front of their eyes. The intensity in those rooms was ten times what you see in the guru video. But nobody had ever thought to put me on camera or to put a mic by my mouth.

That day, I didn't go in there with much planned. I never do. I usually have a general idea of what I'm going to talk about—a subject, a message, an atmosphere—but I don't write it down or practice it ahead of time. Rote learning has never been my thing. I do better when I feel that I can be spontaneous, when I can see what the crowd needs and calibrate my delivery and content to their vibe. However, that day I did have a notecard in my hand. You can see it in the video. It's weird. I never use notecards. It's not me. It's not natural. But, for whatever reason, that day, I had written down a Lance Armstrong quote: "Pain is temporary. It may last a minute, or an hour, or a day, or a year, but eventually it will subside and something else will take its place. If I quit, however, it lasts forever." And when I read it, those kids sat up. (Sometimes people think that's my quote, so, Lance, if you heard about that, I'm sorry, bro. I wasn't trying to steal your wisdom.)

Here's another truth: I don't know why I told the guru story. I hadn't thought of it before I walked into the room that day. I know that a version of it comes from a book I'd read years before, but I don't even remember reading that part of it myself for the first time. And yet there the words were, in my mouth, coming out into that room, traveling through that microphone, being recorded by that video camera. There the story was, traveling into the ears of these young people whose lives and futures were on the line. There it was for the millions upon millions of people who have heard it since.

CJ was in the room that day, too, and he agrees with me. He says it was the same as any other day. And, like every other day, I got those kids' attention. CJ says that when they heard my voice, my intensity, my urgency, it was like their dad or their coach was in there yelling at them. They all looked like they'd gotten into a little bit of trouble. They all shifted in their seats. They all sat up a little straighter.

Aside from the camera, the only other difference was the years of work I'd put in before walking into that classroom. By that point, I was beginning to master my craft. I had a feel for what audiences responded to. I had a feel for what would give people that fire they needed to go to the next level. CJ believes that what made that day special was that my voice and all its depth would be heard by anybody in the world who wanted to hear it.

Once we had the video, we used it for orientations. We showed it to the kids in the Advantage. We had another version that was circulated all around MSU for certain programs and as a sort of commercial for the Advantage. And then our other partner, Karl, had an idea. As we were just getting our own business started outside of the university, CJ heard that there was a place on the internet where people were putting up videos of their kids and their cats. He called Karl, who was doing a bunch of odd jobs for us at the time, told him to see about putting the video up on YouTube. This was back in 2008. YouTube had been around for a few years, but it hadn't caught fire the way you see it now. So Karl started a YouTube page, and posted the "Secret to Success," and forgot about it. At the time, we didn't have marketing in place. We didn't have social media. We just figured it was a good place to archive material we were making.

This spirit of being experimental is also miracle territory. CJ and Karl and I have always been good at being experimental. Early in our careers, we were just throwing stuff at the wall to see what would stick. We were willing to try pretty much anything once, to see if it worked. Being experimental, being willing to try things out, being willing to fail and fail again, and then get up and try again—that's putting yourself in miracle territory. This is how some of the most successful people in the world—scientists, artists, chefs, lawyers—make their greatest achievements. Through the sheer willingness to try something out.

How do you do this in your own life? How do you find the space to open to new territory? There was a time when I wasn't as open to the world, and at some point I didn't have a choice but to open up and see things with new eyes. For me, openness came as a result of not doing things in a conventional way. Difference has its advantages. Openness also came as a result of seeing my mistakes. If you keep doing something the same way and it's still not working, something is wrong with the way you're doing things. If you can recognize this, then you can recognize the opportunity to open yourself to a new way of doing things. You must get comfortable with the feeling of being uncomfortable.

When I got to Michigan State, it was the first time I experienced being a minority. It was uncomfortable. But without that experience I would not have progressed or grown. I wouldn't have been exposed to different ways of learning and teaching. I would not have had the opportunity to soak in new ideas and meet new people. When you get experimental, when you try something new, when you put yourself in new places with new people, big things can happen.

Now watch this: The "Secret to Success" video sat on our page for three years before it really clocked any views. And then one day, someone sent us a link to a video. Giavanni Ruffin, an NFL walk-on hopeful, took the "Secret to Success," cut it up, set it to music, and made a workout montage. In it, you hear my voice, "If you want to succeed . . . as bad as you want to breathe . . . then will you be successful," and you see

Giavanni hitting the weight room, sprinting across a beach, sweating and grinding like a beast. Giavanni hadn't yet been drafted, but he was getting himself into shape to do a couple of practices with any NFL team that called. From what I understand, the video is what would amp him up when he was trying to take it to the next level. The internet was miracle territory. Giavanni's video was the miracle.

Suddenly, the guru story went viral. It got remixed by the rap artist Da' T.R.U.T.H. It got circulated by Floyd Mayweather. I heard a coach mention on ESPN that the Heat listened to it the first year that LeBron won the championship. Other remixes appeared on the internet, and that video just went crazy. A few thousand. Another few thousand. A few hundred more. And then one day CJ called me and said it had hundreds of thousands of views. We couldn't believe it. Giavanni's ingenuity catapulted me to another level. It foretold the next phase of my career. Since then, my voice has become a fixture on national television. It's been set over commercials for Dodge, Dick's Sporting Goods, Goodyear, and TNT's NBA programming. I've done a Super Bowl commercial almost every year since.

For CJ and me, getting involved in social media and developing a digital strategy early on was putting ourselves in miracle territory. We never expected that YouTube or Instagram would be the main platform of messaging for our audience. When we started, Instagram didn't even exist. But in the same way that you must first try to discover your superpower and your gifts, you must first try new things to get into miracle territory. If you never try to play the violin, you don't know if you have the gift of music. If you don't try to play tennis, you don't know if you can hit a mean backhand. If you don't get up and try something new, get yourself out there, you aren't ever going to land in miracle territory.

At some point the guru story became legend. It was a milestone before I recognized it for myself. One day, I looked up and people knew my name because they felt and understood the urgency I was trying to convey to that classroom of kids. They felt it and they used it for their own fuel.

After that day in class, I didn't tell the guru story again. And now I only do it if someone requests it for a seminar. But even then, I ask them, "Why you wanna hear that story again? You already know it. You can go look it up and watch it again and again if you want to." But people like to hear the hits. The important thing to CJ, though, was that I not become a one-hit wonder. So every day, we keep building on what we have. We release new videos, which are each small miracles unto themselves if you think about it. That I can speak to you every week with a new message, and connect to you in your own home, is remarkable.

If you'd told me that telling that story to a classroom full of college students getting ready for midterms would be an inflection point in my career, I wouldn't have believed you. But this is how things happen. You practice and you practice. And then you show up for the game. Look at Steph Curry. He's a little guy from a small school, who just practiced that three-point shot. And then one day, when he appeared on the NBA court, it was like he was a fully formed superstar who had come out of nowhere. But this is how careers are made. It's not magic. You practice and practice, repeat and repeat, make it part of your muscle memory, all when nobody's watching. And then, you play a game, hit all your field goals, make a winning touchdown, and you're suddenly on a different level. Miracles come from practice.

Prepare for Your Miracle, Visualize Your Miracle

So how do you put yourself in miracle territory?

First of all, miracles will come to you when you're being the most you. If you've identified your superpower and are walking along your path of purpose, it means that you are on your way to discovering and honoring your innermost you. But it's important to remember this: When you're seeking opportunities, it's possible that you may feel you have to be a certain thing or act a specific way or perform a kind of role in order to get an opportunity. When you act like somebody else, not only are you betraying yourself, you're signaling to the world that you are not comfortable in your own skin. People can feel this, whether they're conscious of it or not, and will respond to it in kind. But when you're being the most authentic version of yourself, opportunities that are suited to you and your gifts will begin to come to you.

Spend time with people who have witnessed miracles or have been the recipient of miracles. I hang with people who have seen all sorts of miracles and believe in them, too. There is power in hanging with positive people—people who are open to the world are full of curiosity and wonder. If you can talk to people who have seen things bigger than you and bigger than themselves, you can learn from their experiences. It's like gathering advice from native shamans or studying African proverbs about going to different spiritual realms. People who have gone before us into unfamiliar territory are the best models to help us understand what stories and experiences of miracles can look like. If they can get a miracle, you can get a miracle, too.

Opportunities come when you prepare to receive them. When you're practicing your purpose every day, you are putting intention toward receiving opportunities. If you're a writer, you wake up and you write. But you don't just write. You connect with other people who write. You take classes on writing or listen to other writers give talks on the craft of writing. You send your writing to friends and family or other writers to read. Maybe you submit your writing to an agent or a magazine. Maybe you pursue career opportunities that involve writing. By putting yourself in the position to practice your craft and think about your craft and talk about your craft, you are not only putting yourself in the position to receive opportunities, you are creating them.

You have to be prepared for your miracle. Envision yourself receiving the miracle. Act as if your miracle is just around the corner. By practicing your gift and putting yourself in the way of opportunities, you're actively preparing yourself emotionally and spiritually to receive a miracle. But if you can visualize what it looks like and feels like to finally receive it, you're also actively opening your mind up to the territory where miracles take place. Athletes do this all the time. They watch tape. They study other players. They study themselves. They visualize themselves running, passing, making touchdowns, sticking the landing, getting the chip, getting the medal.

When I was struggling academically, to get myself in the mind-set of excelling, I would put on a cap and gown, I would play the graduation music, and, in my mind, I'd walk across the stage to receive my diploma. And then I'd get back to work. Years before we could ever afford to buy the house where my wife and I now live part time in Cali, we went and visited to imagine what life could look like. Before I could afford to buy the car I own now, I went and sat in it to feel what it could be like to own it. When my mother-in-law got cancer, the doctors sent her home to die. But she believed she was going to live until she saw her grandbabies graduate from college. She saw herself in the audience, watching them walk across the stage in their caps and gowns. She put herself in the emotional space to receive a miracle. She prepared herself spiritually and mentally to receive the thing that seemed impossible. That was 2008. My mother-in-law is still alive and she's seen her grandkids graduate. Now she's vowed to see them get married. If you've prepared yourself to receive the miracle, you'll be ready when it comes. You'll know what to do with it.

I take a page out of Axel Foley's book, Eddie Murphy's character in *Beverly Hills Cop*. He had one credential—his badge—but that boy from Detroit had confidence that was out the roof. Everyone assumed that he was what he said he was and that was enough to get him anywhere he wanted to go. When I was coming up, beginning to go to conferences while I was still at Oakwood, I created a media company called Concerned Black Students. I would hit a conference where Dennis Kimbro was speaking, and I'd tell the organizers, yo, I'm with CBS, can I get a few minutes with Dennis? I'd hit a conference where Steve Harvey was onstage and get face time with Steve. Nobody asked questions, and I wasn't being disingenuous. I was just using my creativity to talk to the people I wanted to learn from. I worked my own miracles, putting myself in a position to meet people I wanted to learn from and spending time in places where knowledge was flowing.

In my business, making it to the level of corporate speaking is a big deal. If companies start hiring you to come in and speak to their sales forces and their chief executive officers, you're doing all right. Today I do this all the time—I've worked with Under Armour, AT&T, Rocket Mortgage, and a whole range of Fortune 500 companies. But when I was getting started, I didn't even know how to get into the corporate game. I didn't talk the corporate talk. So I started studying the companies where I wanted to speak, started learning how they got started, who ran them, and where their headquarters were. I started a video series called *Thank God It's Monday* that was meant to motivate working professionals, particularly those in the corporate sphere. Even before I started doing corporate, I started preparing myself to do corporate.

When I finally got my first opportunity, it was in 2012. A young man in Cleveland who worked for a Quicken Loans branch there wanted to bring me into his office to speak to his colleagues about building the culture of their team. The company wouldn't pay for it, so for $5,000, he fronted eight sessions himself, and brought me in to talk to his team over two days.

In the last few minutes of the eighth and final session, a guy named Tony Nuckolls came into the room and heard me talking. At the time, he was the vice president of leadership and training development, the highest-ranking African American man in the company. He approached me afterwards and said that I was a little rough around the edges for corporate, but he liked what I had to say, and liked my natural style. He offered to help give me some advice and training to calibrate my work to corporate. If I did all right, he said, he'd help get me in front of some of the company's higher-ups.

Tony changed everything for me. So much of what I learned about business followed. And when I got my foot in the door at corporate, I unlocked the keys to the kingdom.

The Work

1. Are there moments in life when you feel you were in the right place at the right time? Why were you there? What led to you being in that place at that particular time? What choices led you to be there? How did the choices you made get you to that moment?

2. What are the opportunities you've received that have changed your life? Who are the people who have helped bring you those opportunities? How did you meet these people? How do those people intersect with your life? What kinds of opportunities do they receive?

3. What are the opportunities you would like to receive? Who else has experienced these opportunities—rich or famous people, or folks in your own life? What would you do with these opportunities if you received them?

Challenge: Think about an opportunity you would like to receive. Think about what it would take for you to receive that opportunity. Where would you need to be? Who would you need to meet? What would it look like to receive that opportunity? What would it feel like? Make a list of steps big and small that would close the distance between you and that opportunity. Make a list of people and places that would get you closer to seizing that opportunity. Visualize walking yourself through each step and receiving the opportunity.

CHAPTER

7

Become a Triple Threat

KNOWLEDGE IS THE NEW MONEY.

The African American sociologist, activist, and historian W. E. B. Du Bois wrote an essay that I think about a lot. It's called "The Talented Tenth," and it appears in a book of essays by Black writers called *The Negro Problem*, published in 1903. The "Talented Tenth" refers to the one Black man of every ten who's gained an education and become a leader in his community. He believed that those with the most talent could step forward to represent his people and do the work to uplift the rest of the community. Du Bois argued that for Black Americans to reach their full potential and change the trajectory of their history, a classical education was required. For him, education, rather than physical or industrial labor, was the key. Rather than force, strength, or weapons, Du Bois believed that education was the way to fight the system. For me, the notion of education as the foundation of progress couldn't be more true.

When you have knowledge, you have currency. There is an ATM in your head. And it can take you anywhere you want to go.

In Detroit, the heart of American industry, I grew up believing that my value was wrapped up in my ability to labor. I thought I had to go to work with my hands and body to make something of my life. That's how everybody made a living. But the moment I began experiencing true success in life was the moment I began investing in my intellectual education. When I passed the GED, I suddenly gained a sense of control over my future. Even though it took me twelve years to get a four-year degree at Oakwood, once I finished, I was at another level. After college, I kept pushing my education forward and forward and forward. Today,

155

I'm Dr. Eric Thomas. With a title like that, I have more opportunity than most Americans alive today.

Education is only the first step, though. Du Bois also knew this. You can get an education and do nothing with it. You can get an education and be average. You can get an education, but if you don't express yourself clearly, what good did the learning do? You can get an education, but if you don't excel in your field, why have pursued an education at all? If you study the greats of any field, you will notice that they are all educated, they can all express themselves with a deep, studied proficiency, and they perform in their field with unparalleled excellence.

Martin Luther King Jr. had his PhD at twenty-six. Not only could he express his ideas in a way that moved a nation to action, but he was so excellent that we regard him as one of the most elite speakers to ever walk the earth. Thurgood Marshall went to Howard Law and graduated magna cum laude, an honor reserved for the excellent, and he could express himself by writing opinions on the Supreme Court that shifted American history. Jackie Robinson killed his education at UCLA and was an all-around incredible athlete, but in a time when the color of his skin could have held him back, his excellence propelled him forward to change American sports. Toni Morrison, another Howard graduate, expressed her ideas about what it means to be Black in America through fiction so excellently that it earned her not only a Presidential Medal of Freedom, but a Pulitzer *and* a Nobel Prize as well. She wasn't formally educated, but Sojourner Truth schooled herself in scripture and human rights at a time when Black Americans were thought to be chattel, and expressed herself so effectively that she is remembered today as one of the country's most excellent and important abolitionists.

Education is important, but once you've got the education, it's got to be balanced and activated with expression and excellence. I'm good at what I do because I can express myself clearly. I am excellent because I knew I had to work harder than anyone else to get to the position of world's number one motivational speaker. It doesn't just happen. It takes work. You need to become a triple threat to get to number one. You need to educate yourself. You need to express yourself. And you need to be excellent.

Education Is More Than School; Education Is Knowledge

A lot of kids I work with are apathetic when it comes to school. When I get into a classroom I always ask the same question: How many of y'all hate school?

Almost every time, 90 percent of hands go up.

A lot of young people I work with don't see the value of education because they haven't had a model for what it can do. It's not obvious how the concepts of the classroom translate into real life. Rote learning seems superfluous to survival. What does it matter if a + b = c? Who cares about conjugations and gerunds and subjunctive mood? From the perspective of a kid, it might not be obvious how these sorts of concepts help you express yourself clearly or become excellent in the world. And, as a result of not seeing the connection between these abstract concepts and their value, a lot of young people view education as a waste of time.

But also, growing up, African American kids don't always have the same opportunity to see generations of family who have graduated from high school or college. It's the same for any American who is at a social or economic disadvantage. Since the founding of this country, education hasn't been prioritized for the poorest of our people, and lower-income neighborhoods, towns, and cities suffer from divestment and a lack of re-sources. If your parents and grandparents and great-grandparents didn't finish high school or never went to college, you may not have a model for what the value of education can look like growing up. If you didn't see the way that education could open doors for you, you don't even know what's possible. My mom calls this kind of ignorance triple darkness: You don't know that you don't know that you don't know.

For my community, education is a divisive concept. There was a time in American history when it was illegal for a person of color to read or write. You could be thrown in jail, tortured, beaten, or lynched for becoming literate. When Frederick Douglass learned to read and write, he had to do it secretly and stealthily. He'd practice reading and writing when nobody was looking. He'd get the white kids to help him learn. When Douglass took his education into his own hands, he bought his own freedom. As an educated man, he was treated differently and had greater access to the American dream. Before forging the Underground Railroad, Harriet Tubman went to a preacher who gave her the road map to freedom, and he insisted that she learn how to educate herself so it wouldn't be as obvious that she wasn't free. For the longest time, even after emancipation, Black kids in the South couldn't go to school if it was cotton-picking season. Education for my people started off as a dangerous prospect, and this lingering shadow still breeds skepticism today around why education is worth the trouble.

For my family, and many American families, physical labor has always been a way to make it in the world. If you grew up anywhere near Detroit before 2000, you know what I'm talking about. Your future was working on the line at Ford or GM or Chrysler or some manufacturing plant that supported the auto industry. After emancipation, you could always find the laboring type of work as a Black person. Even when my ancestors came up North in the Great Migration without a hint of what lay ahead of them, they knew they could find work doing some sort of job in a factory, on a construction site, on a farm. The harder you labored the more valuable you were to whoever your master was—plantation owner, contractor, car company. Historically, in my world, more value has been placed on working your body than on working your mind. If you go back in your family's lineage, and you don't see a robust history of schooling, chances are your people were laboring. But as Sojourner Truth said, "It is the mind that makes the body."

Humans perpetuate patterns. My mom barely finished high school. My biological father didn't finish school at all. My grandmother had a third-grade education. My great-grandparents weren't even allowed to learn in the same way my children do today. In my family, the roots of laboring are deep. Education is a newer commodity and confers a newer sense of power for us.

With the kids I spend time with in GED programs or in juvenile detention centers or in communities that don't have adequate resources, I ask them: Do you want the life your parents lived? Do you want the life your grandparents lived? I ask them to think about the reality of those lives—how frustrating it must have been for their parents to work two jobs to take care of them or how exhausting it must have been to come home after hard labor, scrape together rent, and go without certain luxuries just to feed them. Who would choose to struggle? You live in a world today where you have a chance to choose the life you want to live. I tell them: If you want something different, you have think about the life you want to live and then you have to live it.

Treat Your Education Like It's Life or Death

Before Michigan State, I had never operated in a white world. And when I first walked through campus, it hit me. White people everywhere. To make the color line even more stark, somehow all the Black kids ended up at Hubbard Hall, a dorm on the east side of campus. The school said it wasn't on purpose, but we knew what was going on. CJ lived there as an undergrad, and says he didn't mind it—they had their own culture, their own clubs, their own ecosystem apart from the rest of the school. Back then, if you were Black and you were at Michigan State, it's probably because you were an athlete or possibly had some affirmative action working on your side.

For me, landing at MSU was complete and utter culture shock. And not just because everybody was white. The size of the school alone had me reeling. Oakwood had an enrollment of 1,800 students. Michigan State's was 50,000. And then there was the academic rigor. I'm not saying that Black schools are not academically rigorous. You look at someplace like Howard University or the Urban Prep Academy schools in Chicago, and that's some of the best education you can get in America. But a Detroit public school is a totally different thing from a Bloomfield Hills public school. A Crenshaw public school is a world away from a Beverly Hills public school. Not only is the standard of learning on a different plane, but so is the vernacular. At Oakwood, my teachers told Black stories in Black language with Black cues and nuances. When I got to Michigan State, I was a fish out of water. I couldn't understand the reference points or stories or subtle cues of the dominant culture. Eventually, I started hanging out with other Black students and teachers who'd grown up going back and forth, code-switching, who helped me

translate what I was hearing—people like the writer Demetrius Mar-
lowe; Dr. Pero Dagbovie, whose African parents were educators; and Dr.
Chris Dunbar in my master's department—but I was lucky in this respect. Not everybody finds their translators.

At that time, I was a full-grown man, and I'd had plenty of time to
figure out how the world worked. I knew how to find allies and coaches.
I knew how to ask for help. Now imagine being eighteen, a Black kid
from a Black world, showing up to a mostly white campus without a clue
as to how to act. When all you've had is Black and white women teaching you math and history all your life, you don't know how to communicate with university professors who are mostly white and male. And aside
from not speaking the same language, you might not even know you're
supposed to communicate with your professors, period. If you're like
me—a nontraditional learner, let's call it—you haven't necessarily
learned how to use the library or write a research paper or even know to
look at a syllabus to see what was coming next because the word *syllabus*
isn't in your vocabulary. And this phenomenon isn't limited to Black
kids. This is about kids at any kind of disadvantage. This is about kids
who might have learning disabilities or might be physically disabled.
This is about kids whose parents aren't top earners or who grow up with
a single mom or who struggle with emotional or spiritual anxiety. This is
about kids who just walk through the world in a different way.

When I got to MSU, my whole prerogative was to help these kinds of
kids see their way through a predominantly white institution. Like mice
in a maze, they were dropped into an environment they'd never been
taught how to interact with. Going through culture shock myself, I could
empathize with what it was like to come onto campus and feel that you
didn't belong. I looked at these kids, and saw Eric Thomas from twenty

years before. A little apathetic, a lot ignorant, totally unaware of how to study, what it meant to take notes, to ask for help. I saw myself at Oakwood, trying to float through as I had before—on my street smarts and social savvy. I saw the ET who got kicked out, who was told I wasn't cut out for college, who had a wife and a baby son looking at him like he might be a failure. I knew that if these kids couldn't find their way through, they were done for.

When I looked out at these kids and saw myself, I was frightened. I felt an urgency rise up inside me. I felt something grip me and tell me I needed to wake these kids up. I needed to make them feel their own existence, to make them see what kind of opportunity was ahead of them, and that this, *this*, is the moment to take it. I had to convince them that education was the key to unlocking the doors to their entire future. For me, getting them to seize their education felt like life or death.

My first year as an academic adviser at Michigan State I was green. I was idealistic. I was working with these kids, trying to help them make it through the hoops of university life, and I deeply wanted them to make it to the next level. I wanted them to excel without having to go through the decade of struggle I went through, dropping out of high school and then college before figuring out how to navigate my education. I knew I had to change the system of education if anything was going to happen.

So, I started looking into the rates of graduation among Black students at MSU, and what I found shocked me. Black males could only be expected to graduate at a rate of 31.6 percent. That's about three out of ten Black men who matriculate through MSU leaving with actual degrees. Among Black females, the rate was 50 percent. And those estimates are across a six-year career, rather than the standard four. Many of these kids were dropping out after their first year. The other shocking thing I discovered was this: The school could predict exactly who would drop out and when.

This is how it works: When you're a Black kid from the Detroit or Flint or Pontiac public school system and you come to Michigan State, the university can project what your grades are going to be. It's called "predicted GPA." They calculate it based on a whole array of factors. One factor is your high school GPA. But another factor is whether you're from, say, a poor urban community or a wealthy, suburban community. So if you're getting A-pluses at Henry Ford in Detroit, that's like getting C-minuses at Okemos near East Lansing. Predicted GPAs are also based on whether or not your parents went to college, how much money they make every year, and, of course, your standardized test scores. The university knows all this before you even step foot on campus.

So let's say, after assessing all the aspects of your student profile, the university predicts your GPA will be a 1.5 or a 1.2 by the end of your freshman year. That means you're gonna get kicked out of school. Your college career is over. You're going back to Detroit or Flint or Pontiac and you might go to community college or you might get a job at McDonald's or you might fall in with your old friends and get into trouble. Maybe you'll experience some modicum of local success, but you will always wonder what could have been. You will have tasted what it was like to be at one of the best colleges in the country—all that energy, all that opportunity—and then you'll understand what it's like to be without it. And the crazy thing is, the school could have foreseen it—it's a fate ordained from the second you got your acceptance letter—yet the system is set up for you to struggle through and eventually fail.

As a young, idealistic college counselor, seeing these kids getting churned through the system, it just didn't make sense to me that a school wouldn't reach out to help a student whose predicted GPA shows that they're bound to fail. Why would the university admit a student, send them to classes, house them, feed them, give them the opportunity, and then, knowing exactly what direction they're going in, refuse to give them the tools to succeed? I just couldn't understand it.

By gathering all this knowledge for myself, I saw a way to change the system *and* create financial benefit for the university. Of course, the money isn't the point—not for me, anyway—but I knew that a financial incentive would garner the university's support from a bottom-line perspective.

Now watch this: When I discovered that predicted GPAs foretold which students would get kicked out of school, I also calculated that the school was throwing away $50,000 on each student that they had predicted to fail each year. Between housing and paying professors and all the things it takes to support a student through one year of school, this is what it costs the university. However, it's a number that's easy to overlook, since most of the resources are focused on 93 percent of the student population. At the time, less than 7 percent of the students were kids of color, and less than 4 percent of those were Black. I figured if I could help seven kids a year, I could change that graduation rate by 1 percent. If I'm helping seven kids a year, I'm saving the university $350,000. If I could help forty-nine kids, I could change the graduation rate by 7 percent. That's $2.45 million a year saved. Now think of that over the course of five years, ten years. That was evidence enough to convince Michigan State that my counseling program would not only keep these kids in school and create successful students and future MSU ambassadors, but it would also save the university a massive amount of cash in the meantime. It seems like an obvious solution, but the system doesn't always see the obvious, especially when its foundations are built on a system of inequity.

Fall in Love with Learning

My first year of college, someone suggested I should read Ben Carson's book *Gifted Hands*. Carson is from Detroit, spent a large part of his childhood without much of a relationship with his biological father, and had a difficult time in school. He wrote about streets I knew in Detroit. He wrote about growing up as a Seventh-Day Adventist. He wrote about how hard it was to catch up in school, about how he was impulsive and had issues with anger and darkness. I felt like I could see myself in those pages. At the time, I was geographically in college, but I wasn't necessarily intellectually engaged. When I saw myself reflected in Carson's book, and read about his path to becoming one of the country's best neurosurgeons, it stirred something in me. It showed me that education wasn't just for scholars or the wealthy. It showed me that education was a means to freedom and changing your circumstances. Though I may not agree with his political ideologies today, I can say that Carson's book helped me fall in love with learning.

After that, I read every self-help and personal development book I could get my hands on. Og Mandino's *Greatest Salesman in the World*, George S. Clason's *Richest Man in Babylon*, M. Scott Peck's *The Road Less Traveled*. I read Dennis Kimbro, Zig Ziglar, Les Brown. I was in Barnes & Noble on the reg, hitting the library, reading a book a week. I started looking up words in the dictionary, using a thesaurus, studying language. Just like that, I'd become engaged with a whole new world of knowledge.

When I fell in love with learning, I began to embrace education. When I started to seek knowledge beyond what the institution required of me, I fell in love. I fell in love with learning and I fell in love with myself. Learning isn't about some ideology or some concept housed in books on a shelf. Learning is a tool for discovery about the world. Learning is a tool for discovery of yourself. Learning is a tool for demystifying how the world around you works.

When you embrace your education, you start to make connections to the rest of your life. When I discovered what my gift was and realized that it was something I needed to practice to master, I studied it and practiced the way a basketball player might watch tape. I studied the people who forged the field. I studied the people who changed the field. I studied how people responded to the greats and what influence they had over their audiences. From there, I got into the psychological side of speaking—how different tones and body language affect an audience. I studied how the brain processes communication, how to break down concepts for adolescents as opposed to adults, which teaching methods are best for which kinds of learners. To better understand my gift, I started taking classes in sociology and educational systems. I knew I had a gift, but to take it to the next level I needed to grasp the theory behind it. The theory began to help me make connections between my own speaking style and how I could be more effective in communicating to all different kinds of people. Learning the theory and systems behind your gift is the equivalent of going to the weight room to build muscle. It refines things, sharpens things, makes your mind work in a more synergetic way.

When you embrace education, you begin to see opportunities that were seemingly not there before. Because you now have a working knowledge of what is available to you in the world, you can see jobs and people and places that you may never have realized existed in the first place. When I was a high school dropout, I knew about the opportunities in front of me: a job at McDonald's, a friend's couch to sleep on, maybe a job at Ford or GM if I got my act together. Because I wasn't trying to gain knowledge, I had no idea that a place like Oakwood existed. I barely knew the history of my people, let alone had heard of an HBCU before. Opportunities were not available to me then because I wasn't actively seeking knowledge about them. I didn't know that I didn't know that I didn't know.

Fall in love with the process and the results will come.

When I got to Oakwood and began taking classes, the world opened up to me in a way that I'd never known was possible. Eventually, when I got my education on track, I realized that the world would keep unfolding, and revealing opportunities to me if I kept myself hungry to learn. I saw that opportunities would become greater and deeper with my own personal investment. If I had a bachelor's degree, I knew I could get a master's. I knew if I got a master's I could get a permanent position teaching at a university. I knew if I got a PhD, I could sit at the table and help change the whole university system.

Maybe you have a gift for taking electronics apart and putting them back together again. If you just tinker around the house, taking toasters and computers apart and putting them back together again, you're never going to know how that interest and ability can be turned into a purpose. But if you get curious and look into a class on mechanics, or read a book about a famous engineer, or watch a documentary about how computers changed the trajectory of global history, you'll have a sense of which opportunities are available for you and your gift.

Learning, for me, was an act of self-love. It was a way to discover how to be more myself. It was the thing that equipped me to feel comfortable inside my community and out. It gave me the control I needed to move through the world with confidence. It continues to be an investment in myself and my future and my legacy. Yes, I have a PhD, but I continue taking Spanish lessons every day and always have a stack of books I am reading through. I study my craft every day in pursuit of being the best in the world. Not only is learning a way to better yourself, but it enables you to hone your gifts and your purpose, and to better the world around you—your children, your legacy, your field.

It took me nearly forty years to get my full education (you can see now why having a why as your fuel is so important). At any point along the way, I could have easily let the victim mentality hold me down and keep me in a place of paralysis or rejected the difficulty of continuing on the path of purpose. But each time things got hard, I took hold of my why—my family, my people, my ministry—and used it as the fuel to keep going.

Your Mind Is the Tool; Education Is the Sharpening Stone

No matter who you are, education and knowledge are necessary to get to the next level of whatever your gift is. Gathering that knowledge is a major step in walking in your purpose. Even if you're a natural-born genius, you require education to be shaped and to sharpen your skills to superhero-level status. Consider your mind the tool and education the sharpening stone.

When I work with athletes who have all the talent in the world, education can seem superfluous to a professional athletic career. But if you want to be in the NBA, unless you go overseas or are in the G League, it is still the easiest route to go through the college system, at least for one year. And to get into college, you've got to take the SAT or the ACT and have decent grades in high school. And the college you go to matters. If you want to get scouted, you have to go to the D1 schools—the Dukes, the Baylors, the Kentuckys, the USCs—and to get into those schools you have to be excellent beyond just your stats. Education is the first key to your excellence.

Once they get to the pros, athletes don't necessarily need to focus on education to get to the next step, but, in the long run, advancing your knowledge in any respect affects every other part of your life. Yes, as a beast of an athlete, you can get to the next level of your career by simply being fast and strong, but what refines physical skill is mental sharpness. What gets you better endorsements, more substantial paychecks, a platform to share your message is the ability to express yourself. And expressing yourself requires learning—and learning about yourself. ESPN isn't going to put you in front of the camera if you can't talk articulately about what you just experienced in the game. Reporters and writers ain't gonna hit you up if you can't give them a smart quote about how you play or prepare.

But what happens when the cameras get turned off? What happens after you make it to the NFL and your career is over by age twenty-five? What are you going to do with your life? If you don't have an education, if you haven't spent time studying something beyond your sport, you're going to be left behind. You're going to talk like an eighteen-year-old all your life because you haven't expanded your mind. You're going to have the opportunities of an eighteen-year-old because you haven't worked on your business acumen or thought about how to invest in your own brain beyond your body. What does scoring touchdowns have to do with the balance of your life?

As an athlete's body changes and grows older, mental and intellectual abilities become even more important to overall performance. When I started working with quarterback Cam Newton, he had just gotten traded to the New England Patriots. Cam is one of those dudes who has always had a lot of energy and passion. He's always been a physical specimen—his height, his structure, the boy is a beast. All his life he's been superior to the average athlete. As a quarterback, he could always outrun, out-throw, and take hits better than most in his business. But as he's gotten older, his body has changed. When I work with athletes who are coming to terms with the deterioration of their physical abilities, I urge them to transition their excellence toward their mental and intellectual abilities. For Cam, I asked him to focus on being more cerebral.

Perhaps he gets more thoughtful about when he runs the ball as opposed to passing or handing off. Cam's brilliance is in his intuition, so I work with him to push past the impulse of intuition and become more methodical and strategic. In terms of personality types, I work with him to get closer to his Air Traffic Controller—the cautious, strategic, organized part of his personality—and to put his Flight Attendant in check—the more interactive, impulsive side of himself. Constantly learning is key to understanding your mental agility and being able to transition and adapt when conditions change.

At some point, no matter what league you're in, you'll have to look toward what comes after your first profession. Look at somebody like Kareem Abdul-Jabbar. The NBA's all-time high scorer, a nineteen-time All-Star, a six-time MVP, and one of the fifty greatest basketball players ever. After leaving the league, Kareem coached, made movies, became a critically acclaimed writer, and a speaker. He's been awarded the Presidential Medal of Freedom. The man has had a prolific career that is entirely separate from his excellence as an athlete. After an unusually long career (twenty years pro, retired at the age of forty-two), he went on to make a name for himself as an intellectual and a creative.

Grant Hill, one of the NBA's best, went on to become a television host on CBS and an owner of the Atlanta Hawks. He's an art collector, a philanthropist, and is super politically active. Shaquille O'Neal is a sports analyst, an investor, a television personality, and he's had dozens of major endorsements. LeBron James is an activist, a philanthropist, an actor, the owner of his own media company, and has more endorsements than anyone else in professional sports—and he hasn't even retired yet. These are people who are constantly educating themselves, who are looking beyond their identity as athletes, who are creating new modes of expression and income and influence, all while performing at their highest level.

Knowledge Gives You Control over Your Life

Knowledge is the new money. Get you some. You were born with a gift, which means you were born with an ATM machine in your head. All roads to success go through knowledge. You don't need a master's or a PhD, but you do need knowledge. Knowledge is what gives you control over your life.

Though education is the key, it doesn't always have to be formal school learning. It doesn't need to mean chasing after degrees. Education can mean educating yourself on the rules of the game so that you can play the game successfully. If you can survive in the game, you can strive, and if you can strive, you can thrive. The only way to gain control and keep control is through knowing how the world around you works. The only way to combat the system or get beyond the system or change the system, it is to study the system.

Take Muhammad Ali. He is still called "The Greatest." His mother was a domestic worker and his dad was a sign painter. Ali was dyslexic and didn't have a great command of reading and writing. He went to high school, but he didn't go to college. Did he need to get a degree to become The Greatest? He went from Cassius Clay to Muhammad Ali to become the The Greatest because he took control of his situation. He studied Islam with individuals like Elijah Muhammad and Malcolm X to become knowledgeable about his spirituality. He learned about the trajectory of American culture, how capitalism had enslaved his people, and how Christianity as a Eurocentric religion fed into the colonizers' mentality. He educated himself on how the system worked and he worked the system. When he was drafted into the military, he understood that if he took a stand against the system with the knowledge he had, he could beat it. And he did.

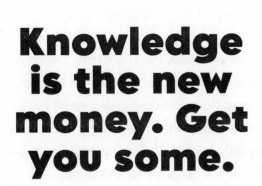

Knowledge is the new money. Get you some.

If you can't get to school or afford to take that next step in your education quite yet, you have so many other tools at your disposal. You can go to the library. If you aren't great at reading, you can listen to audiobooks. If you've got a phone in your hand, you have literally all the knowledge in the world at your fingertips. If you have an interest in something, start researching it. Find people who know about it. Call or write them and see if they'll talk to you. Get on online forums and see if people are talking about the thing you want to know about. Ask questions. Get curious. You aren't getting any knowledge if you don't act as if you want to know about it. Knowledge has never been easier to access than at this moment in history.

Expression Gives You Control of How You Operate in the World

No matter what your level of education, expression is necessary to leveling up.

When I was young, I had what they call the "gift of gab" from the time I could open my mouth. I just liked to be around people and I liked to talk about anything. I was invited to start speaking at Detroit Center and discovered that this was indeed a gift beyond just an impulse. And I started to understand that structuring this gift was necessary to harness its power. Nobody tells you this as a kid, but structure is divine. Boundaries are a beautiful thing. Everybody needs structure and boundaries to express themselves.

Expression is education and knowledge within the boundaries of structure. Once I realized that I could express my gift within the parameters of a sermon at Detroit Center or a message at Bell Tower, I found that I could apply what I was learning at the same time.

Education and expression are deeply linked. It's imperative to learn about your gift so you can express yourself. In my work, expression is the whole point. Everything depends on how clearly I can express myself and how deeply I can connect to people through that expression. I've always had a knack for talking, so when I first began to speak at church and at Bell Tower, I spoke from the gut. I had an intuition of what I needed to do by mimicking the greats before me: Martin Luther King

Jr., Jessie Jackson, Maya Angelou, Marcus Garvey. With the raw gift of my voice, I turned heads, but I wasn't necessarily sharp.

I had never really taken words seriously, and for a person whose career depends on stringing words together to make an impact on audiences, I was in dire need of some schooling. I would hear someone use a word in a sentence and deduce what it meant from that sentence, but I couldn't apply it to other sentences. When I finally put my mind to learning vocabulary and definitions, I realized that I had a new control over words and could deploy them whenever it was appropriate. My dyslexia added to the issue. I was phonetically challenged, so I had a difficult time with words that looked different from how they sounded—like *chaos* or *cough* or *knot*. I struggled with homonyms—words that have the same pronunciation, but different meanings, like *bear* and *bare* and *here* and *hear*. I struggled with things like the difference between *to* and *too* and *two*. But once I learned a pronunciation or the rule behind a word's use, I got confident in using those jokers. I felt that I had power when I started writing a research paper and could move them around any way I wanted to. The more I practiced, the more I felt in control of the way I related to the world around me.

Code-Switching Is a Natural Part of Expression

I've found that the most effective orators from our community are the ones who have been able to express themselves to broad audiences. They're the ones who can capture the attention and imagination of people of all ages, races, genders, and politics. They're the ones who have gathered an audience beyond the block, beyond the neighborhood, beyond the city. They're the ones who have moved nations. And while they became comfortable code-switching, depending on their audience, they also never forgot where they came from. Frederick Douglass. Barack Obama. Nelson Mandela. Jesse Jackson. Oprah Winfrey. MLK Jr.

There was a time that I could only speak to the African American community because I only knew the language and the rules of the African American community. But now I'm able to appeal to everybody. Because I also started learning the language and the rules of the world.

If you don't look outside your world, you're only going to be able to express yourself within the world you live in. I know the code with my people is deep. And sometimes, if you break it, you pay the price. I think a lot about Yummy Sandifer. I'll never forget seeing that little boy's face on the cover of *Time* magazine back in 1994. I was at the Boys & Girls Club in Atlanta doing some volunteer work, and when I picked it up, I knew exactly who he was. I grew up with kids like him. He had those dookie braids down the back of his head, looking up at the camera like he was tough. He was only eight when he started stealing stuff and joined a gang in his Chicago neighborhood. He was eleven when he got orders to kill some people. And when the gang thought he'd turned on them—that he'd snitched and broken the code—they executed him. Wherever I go, I work with kids like Yummy. Kids who are from a certain neighborhood or block. Kids who are perpetuating a pattern of behavior because they don't know any better. I see kids all over from all sorts of places who grow up thinking that their world is the only world that exists, and there's nothing better or different on the other side of it. They know the code and the language of that one place, and that's all they've got.

This is heavy stuff, but it's stuff I think about. I think about how we cancel our own because of a certain code. I think about how little boys like Yummy grow up in a system that they don't even know they're part of. I think about how sometimes the code can hold you back or keep you in the same place or even kill you. I remember feeling embarrassed to tell my boys in Detroit that I was studying to get a GED. I remember feeling that I had to keep the fact that I was going to Oakwood a secret sometimes. I remember feeling that I was betraying the place I came from when I started learning new things. Knowing a code can open up certain aspects of life, but the same code doesn't work for all locks.

When I got to Oakwood, I learned all sorts of new ways to express myself—academically, culturally, through my faith. At Michigan State I learned new levels of expression by being in a predominantly white environment. In both cases, I saw that I had an option to maintain my own mode of expression or to level up so I could communicate with the people around me. If you can't speak Spanish, you can't go to Spain or Latin America and understand the nuances of a culture. If you don't know the language of academics, you can't go to a university and get the full benefit of being there. I started studying how professors talked and how they relayed their message. I sat in my lectures with the specific goal of absorbing cadence and tone and sentence structure. Soon I could write papers and articulate myself to a lecture hall full of students in the language of the academy. I could interact with a new world in a new way and see how I fit into it in ways I never knew were possible.

Even though I have learned additional languages, I have never forgotten my native tongue. It's blended with the words and structures I've learned out in the world. They've all come together in a way that only my brain could reformulate, and changed the way that I see the world. I like to think it's changed the way the world sees me, too.

This is how we grow and advance as humans. We learn new words. We deepen our understanding of the way we relate to the world around us. As teenagers, we do not speak the same way we spoke when we were children. As adults, we do not speak the same way we spoke when we were teenagers. We gain new vocabulary. Our sentences become more complex. We can express nuance and infer meaning. We can create allusions and metaphors and invent words all our own. We can abstract and clarify and compound in infinite ways. The shifting and manipulation of language is the very premise of poetry and hip-hop. As people of the world, as people dedicated to learning, we gain new knowledge and in doing so we deepen and layer our modes of expression.

W. E. B. Du Bois wrote about double consciousness. It's the idea that we will always see ourselves through the lens of our oppressors. Today, the theory can be applied to anyone living in a society who experiences social inequality and the damaging effects of dominant power structures. People argued with Du Bois that he was playing into the dominant system by believing that to be excellent, you needed to obtain a classical education. But what Du Bois knew was that in order to subvert and change the system, you had to know the language of the system. You can't hack a computer if you don't know how to read and write code.

Martin Luther King Jr. had a PhD. My man knew the Queen's English. But he never lost his identity. He walked among his people. But he knew he would need to code-switch to be able to speak to white culture on behalf of his people. The greater command MLK had over language, the greater command he had over his influence in the world. And he used his influence to create change for his people.

Sometimes people in the Black community will say to me, "Yo, E. Why you talking so white? You selling out." But code-switching is part of my job, and I do what I do for my people. One of my deepest whys is to create change for and make more and better opportunities for my people. As W. E. B. Du Bois believed, I want to be a representative of my community to move our culture and our status forward. I am certain that a major part of my success has to do with remaining true to my roots. I've broken glass ceilings in my business, and created new audiences for a field that has traditionally been all about white men who aspire to wealth and power. Along with it, I've attracted people from all walks of life. By speaking to my community, my messages have resonated with all kinds of underdogs and outsiders and people who have been made to feel that the system was not built for them. By expressing myself in the way that only I, ET, can express myself, I have transcended boundaries that my ancestors couldn't have imagined transcending.

If you can express yourself and do it excellently, the world will listen. If you are true to yourself and honor the place you came from, the world will listen. I am who I am because of where I come from. I am who I am because of the experiences I've gone through. It's all woven into the language I use and the way I move in a crowd. If you see me speak in a locker room or in a foster home or in a corporate office or at an event in London, you know where I am from. You can hear what I've seen. When you hear me open my mouth, no matter who you are or where you are in the world, you can understand me and connect to me and feel something move deep inside you. And that is the power of expression.

Even if you think you don't do it, code-switching is something everyone does every day. We communicate differently with every single person we know. The codes we use might appear similar, but when modulated a certain way, their final expression is altogether different. When your mom calls you on the phone, you talk to her differently than you talk to your best friend. When you talk to your husband or wife, you use different words and tones than you do with your coworkers. When you interact with your kids, you use a different pitch and vocabulary than you do with their teachers.

Code-switching is natural and it's necessary. If you have any self-awareness, you adapt to your surroundings, including the people in them. You act differently in a museum than you do at an NFL game. I used to acclimate intuitively, without much deep thought. But now that I know different languages, I think analytically about when to deploy them.

When I started doing corporate work at Quicken Loans, I had to learn how to talk the talk. The first thing my boy Tony Nuckolls did was put me in corporate meeting rooms so I could get a feel for the difference between inspirational speaking and the language of corporate training. I watched him do his thing—run meetings, give instruction, delegate tasks—and just soaked up how the environment worked. I took notes on the industry lingo and how people responded to certain messages. The next thing he schooled me on was analyzing a company's values. To talk to corporate executives, you need to go in with a full understanding of the corporation's mission statement, its culture, its philosophy. You have to be able to digest all that and infuse it into your own presentation. Tony also taught me how to be brief. If you let me, I'll speak for ten minutes on one point. But Tony could say the same thing in one minute without losing any of the meaning. In fact, his one-minute speech would be twice as impactful. He got me on track with what people in the industry were reading and how I could incorporate that into my own work and messages. And then he gave me insight into what kinds of programs were financially valued. If you can build follow-up programming and analysis into your work beyond the main speaking event, the value of your presence increases. By hanging with Tony, I gained a whole new language and a perspective on a world I knew existed, but hadn't broken into.

What I learned from my man Tony is that the calibration of language to an audience can open up new doors and manifest new opportunities in ways I never imagined. When I began to infuse certain messages, especially TGIM, with the language of the corporate world, I started to get calls from all over the place. Corporations started flying me in first-class for conferences, putting me up in beautiful hotel suites, flying my family out to stay with me, and picking up my tab while I was on their time. My videos became staples of corporate sales forces all across the country. Guys come up to me all the time and tell me they use my work to pump them up before they hit the streets or make calls or take meetings. With a little bit of adjustment and fine-tuning, expression becomes an incredibly powerful tool that can reach audiences you never knew you could have.

Learn Your Own Language

What kind of expression do you need to take it to the next level? First, you need to survey the worlds you're trying to live in and evaluate the language used in those worlds. If you're a teacher, there's the language of pedagogy. If you're a lawyer, you speak the language of law. If you're a doctor, there's the language of medicine. Every field has its own specialized language, and as you begin to internalize this language, you also begin to internalize that world's culture and values.

What's important to remember in the process of learning new languages is that you need to remain true to your own personal language. When we adopt new patterns of speech and new ideas about the world, we sometimes let these things supersede our original modes of expression. But the greatest among us—the people we remember for their singular way of expressing themselves—are the ones who have taken what they've learned, fused it together with their own language, and come out sounding like nobody else in the world.

Muhammad Ali, despite his learning disability, found a new way to express himself through language that moved crowds and imprinted itself upon history: Float like a butterfly, sting like a bee. Huey Newton, despite not knowing how to read, taught himself Plato and eventually got a PhD in philosophy. Because of his unique background and his way of mixing up language, his speeches sounded like nobody else in this world. Kanye West may be a college dropout, but his mom was the chair of the English department at Chicago State University. That boy lived in a kind of school, absorbing rhythms and language and reformulating it into the art he's made over the last twenty years. 2Pac might not have finished high school or gone to college, but he picked up on his mother's experiences from the Black Panthers, and blended that knowledge with where he was from, plus he had a command of language that made him a rarity even among artists.

For me, I've always felt my language has been influenced by the sounds of Detroit. I grew up around Motown and gospel. It was Michael Jackson, Marvin Gaye, and James Brown. Aretha and Mahalia Jackson. Later it was all the hip-hop coming out of the '80s and '90s. And as their music progressed, so did I. I listened to the ways they wove political and social issues through their lyrics, how they went from one style to another as they got older. I soaked up all the rhythms and the cadences, and sometimes my talks come out sounding like music today.

Once you've found your method of expression, study it, practice it, refine it. Keep what serves you, and get rid of what's superfluous. Work on your weaknesses. Change up your environment. Put yourself in front of new audiences. Consistently evaluate yourself. Ask yourself what you're trying to express and how best to do it. Try new modes of expression. Stay true to the modes that make you feel most you, and connect them to the modes that will get you to the next level. Just because I do corporate gigs doesn't mean I speak like the marketing director of an insurance company. It means that I fuse the language of corporations with my own sense of language, and deploy that mode of expression when the occasion calls for it.

Practice doesn't make perfect. Practice makes permanence.

Today, if you look at the progression of my videos, you can see that the way I express myself is clearer, sharper, and more pointed than when I first began. Because I keep studying and learning, my expression becomes clearer and clearer. I still work on my ability to express myself at the highest level possible and to all kinds of different people.

Expression isn't always verbal, of course. Expression is the manifestation of all kinds of languages—spiritual, physical, intellectual. Artists express themselves through painting and sculpture and drawing. Dancers express themselves through choreography and movement. Musicians through chords and symphonies. Writers write. Singers sing. Athletes leap and run and catch and throw. Of course, I express myself through speaking. The greats are the ones who continue to gather knowledge—continue studying painting technique, continue challenging their bodies, learning new songs, writing deeper books. They're also the ones who apply structure to their knowledge. Expression can be simple or complex. It can be direct or abstract. Expression can come in many forms. But when it's done at the highest level, it is studied and it is structured. Every single great is remembered for their ability to express knowledge at a level that is singular and excellent.

Excellence Is Expression in Its Clearest Form

Education and expression are a complete package when they are executed with excellence. Excellence is what comes from translating your education and knowledge into their clearest, most affecting form of expression.

What's the point of being excellent if you have your education and you can express yourself clearly? Why push yourself to excel? The Bible says that the man who is diligent in his work will stand before kings. Very simply, the opportunities that you get when you are excellent are greater than the opportunities you get when you are merely average. The way you experience the world when you are excellent is vastly different from the way you experience it when you're operating at a level of mediocrity.

To illustrate the power of excellence, I like to tell the story of a kid named Jay who worked at Best Buy. He worked on the floor and at the register, and he gave 120 at his job. People came in looking for a remote or a speaker, and Jay gave it everything. Someone needed to check out, and he was friendlier and more enthusiastic than anyone else. One day, an exec from Quicken Loans came in when Jay was working the register. Jay helped that guy out the way he helped everybody—excellently. The exec saw Jay's potential, saw how he was giving everything he had to that job, and invited him to come work at the company. Just from doing his job as a regular employee at a big box store with everything he had, he opened a door of opportunity that would never have been available to him otherwise. Today Jay is a best-selling rep out in Phoenix. The guy is killing it.

When you're excellent, you can fly above the world in a different way. You gain freedoms and see things with a higher-level perspective. You don't get bogged down in the mind-set of the victim because you possess the knowledge that you are responsible for your own success. Being excellent is about being ready to receive your success when it comes to you.

You Have to Want Excellence

When we talk about excellence in the Black community, we talk about Black excellence. It's not just about working hard, it's about working harder than anybody else to get to the next level. It's the same for anyone who might be at a social disadvantage. In many cases, women have to work twice as hard as men to make the same money. Older people have fewer opportunities at jobs than younger people. People with disabilities don't have the same open doors that people without disabilities do. If you come from an oppressed group of people—age, race, gender, economic, or otherwise—not only are you required to overcome your circumstances with fewer resources, but you have to do it better than everybody else. You can't just be average. You have to be excellent. Maya Angelou says it best: "Nothing will work unless you do."

The way I see this is simple: My people who came before me just didn't have the opportunities that I have. Even though it might be harder for me to make the same paycheck or get the same job as somebody in my position who has greater advantages, my only choice is to be excellent and grind harder and longer. If there's an extra mountain to climb, climb it. If there's another degree you need to have, go get it.

The first step to excellence is the desire. You have to want to be excellent. The average person doesn't even make it to this step. The average person studies people who are excellent and admires them from afar. They don't make the connection that the capacity for excellence resides within. The person who desires excellence, who can see that they have the ability to become so, is the person who exceeds expectations over and over again to become greater than the average human.

The next step to excellence is identifying what you want to excel at. This, of course, is connected to your superpower and your path of purpose. Whatever you're good at, you have the ability to be excellent in. I knew I was always good at service. I loved making people happy. Even when I was homeless, I got to work and put a smile on my face, and did the absolute best I could do that day. Because I was working in my superpower, working in excellence felt like second nature. That said, why not be excellent at everything you do? If you're a husband, be an excellent husband. If you're a student, be an excellent student. If you're a parent, be an excellent parent. Excellence is not limited to careers or jobs or vocations.

Get obsessed with what you want to excel at. To be excellent, you have to be like the Michael Jordans and the Kobe Bryants—insatiable, irrepressible, insane. The truly excellent among us know that we will wake up every day in pursuit of a perfection that cannot be reached. We wake up every day seeking to be better than we were the day before. We wake up every day with the goal of improving and moving forward toward greatness.

Excellence is a matter of practice, and learning is a structured way to practice. When I started teaching, I read books on personal growth and development. Athletes watch tape and study the greats who came before them so they might incorporate those moves into their own game. Artists study art history. They study the painting and sculpting of the great masters so they can build it into their own base of knowledge. Doctors study immunizations and neuroscience and surgery—all the techniques that were forged as the field progressed—so they can advance their own understanding of how to help their patients. If you want to be able to express your gift, you have to fully understand its complexity.

The next step to excellence is creating a system of self-evaluation. You can't be satisfied if you're not performing at the highest level. You can't lie to yourself and let yourself get away with only giving 80 percent. I have always known when I am not giving my best. When I was getting fired from jobs or getting in trouble in school, I was always aware that I was shortchanging myself, and I always felt the consequences of my lack of effort doubly.

I start with a benchmark. I personally define what excellence means to me—as a husband, as a father, as a speaker. I ask myself: What does excellence look like? I create a mental picture of what that should mean. When I wake up, I ask myself as I'm moving forward, *Am I being excellent or just average?* I break the idea of a benchmark down into three things: a certain skill level, an attitude, and effort.

Identify your skill. Is it shooting threes? Is it balancing a business's books? Is it communicating among departments at your job? Ask yourself how people are impacted by your skill and what that means to you. Then ask yourself what your attitude is about executing that skill. Do you wake up every day excited to work on it? Or do you get down when you think about working on that skill? If it's the latter, think about what it is that gets you down and try something different. When it comes to effort, ask yourself what kind of effort you are putting forth. Evaluate your own work, but also ask yourself how the people closest to you are affected by your work. Ask your boss, your wife, your kids, what the metrics are. Ask them if you are holding your own. Ask them if you are spending enough time with them. Don't be afraid to let other people in your life weigh in. Lastly, ask yourself what type of progress you want to make in your skill. Have you been performing excellently for six months but not growing? Or are you growing a little every day? Communicating better every day? Reading more every day? Getting faster every day? If you grow 1 percent a day, at the end of the year, you'll have grown 365 percent. Evaluate your progress week to week, month to month, quarter to quarter, year to year.

Excellence is a matter of consciousness within. At the end of the day, you're not competing with anyone else when you're committed to excellence. Excellence is deeply related to your why in life. When you have a why, you have fuel that keeps you moving toward excellence. Whatever you're doing, you're doing it for you and for your why—not to receive a reward. Excellence is never about being rich or famous. It is never for the extrinsic things. I don't wear watches. I don't drive fancy cars. I don't wear gold chains or jewelry. I've lived in the same house for over fifteen years. I am the best at what I do because I have something inside me that is bigger than living like a billionaire. It's bigger than winning. It's bigger than getting validation from other people. I have something inside me that outweighs everything external and drives me to be the most excellent I can be when I wake up each day.

The only way to get out of mediocrity is to keep shooting for excellence.

It's not uncommon for people to slide backward after hitting peak performance. As I move through my own experience of excellence, I constantly adjust and move the bar forward. Once I reach a benchmark,

I look toward the next one. Once I had my bachelor's degree, I looked forward to my master's. Once I had the master's, it was the PhD. Now I'm after the Nobel Prize.

The Work

1. What is your attitude toward education? What is your attitude toward learning? What is your attitude toward knowledge? Dig into each of these answers and try to uncover where the source of your attitude came from.

2. Are you naturally curious? If you have a question about something, do you try to find the answer? Why or why not? What is it that pushes you to find the answer? If not, what stops you from wanting to know the answer?

3. How do you best express yourself? With the written word? With your physical gestures? With speaking? With drawing? In what ways do you struggle to express yourself? When you struggle, what is it you struggle with? How do you react to this struggle?

4. When you think about using your gifts, do you exert yourself in a way that feels all-consuming? Do you ever hold back from exerting your gifts? Do you feel like you have more to give when you are practicing your gifts? If so, what is it that holds you back?

Challenge: Think about something you would like to learn about that pertains to your gifts. Set aside time to research it. While you're researching it, become aware of how you feel about the act of getting to know it. What's happening in your body? What's happening in your mind? Spend time with these feelings. Once you've done some learning and spent time with how you feel about it, take that newfound knowledge and attempt to express it however you best express yourself. Have a conversation with someone about it. Write about it. Paint about it. Dance about it. How does this expression feel? Could it get cleaner? More precise? Do you need to learn a little bit more? Could you practice it? Could you change the mode of expression or blend it with another? How can you communicate it so that it will capture attention and turn heads? How can you express it without holding anything back while still remaining clear? Spend time with your new knowledge and build on it a little bit every day. Put effort toward cultivating it. Put effort into expressing it a little bit more clearly each day. Make notes of your progress and how progressing makes you feel.

Sacrifice Good for Great

GOOD IS GOOD, BUT GOOD IS NOT GREAT.

I will never forget the advice that Pastor James Doggette, who led our church group in Huntsville, gave me the year before we left for MSU. He told me that speaking professionally without a degree in my twenties was cute, but that when I hit thirty, doors would start to close. When that time came, I would reach my ceiling for success. He put it into my mind that to protect the life I had, I couldn't just keep doing the same thing over and over again. I needed to grow up and expand my ideas of what it meant to succeed. Because what doesn't grow, dies.

There was no guarantee that when I got to Michigan State I would get a permanent teaching position. There was no guarantee that I wouldn't have the same difficulties with school that I'd had before. There was no guarantee that we'd build the same community and the same following we'd had in Huntsville. Nothing about giving up what we had was in exchange for something tangible or guaranteed. But I knew that I had to risk it. I couldn't be afraid of what was ahead just to keep holding on to what I had.

This way of thinking changed the way I move through life now. Walking in my purpose gained new depth and meaning. Walking in my purpose meant walking forward, advancing, dreaming forward. It meant cultivating a constant hunger for learning, for never being satisfied with what was set before me. When you keep doing the same workout over and over again, your body gets used to it. You stop feeling sore. You stop losing weight. Parts of your body get overdeveloped while other parts lose definition and muscle. This is what happens to your mind and your spirituality and your emotional well-being when you stay in the same place.

When you stop progressing, you lose your edge. But when you're always hungry, always stretching your capacity, you're always moving forward.

The way I saw leaving Huntsville was like this: Everything has an expiration date. Bread that's fresh today is stale tomorrow. Milk that's good today is sour the next. What's good in your twenties is not necessarily what's good in your thirties. The things that satisfy you today may not be what satisfy your desires next year. The life that Dede and I had built in Huntsville over the course of ten years was part of a dream we had conceived of as teenagers. And to keep moving forward, to build on our dream, we had to keep dreaming bigger. What we had was good. But I wanted something great.

Agitation Can Push You to Be Great

But what happens when you're involuntarily pushed out of something you consider good? What happens if you have something good, and you're forced to leave it behind—a job, a spouse, a city? Whether you can take that experience and transform it into something great depends on you.

Athletes are constantly being traded. Every day they reevaluate their bodies, their teams, their futures. Part of the business of being an athlete is getting traded, moving to new teams, working with new coaches and players. I tell my guys that getting traded is the best position to be in. Getting let go is an opportunity to see the world with new eyes.

You might have won a championship or two Super Bowls and then start to get lax because you've already felt what it's like to be a winner. But when someone trades you, you feel a fire you haven't felt in years because you want to show your old team that they're missing out on your talents. Getting traded can push a player forward. You can stay on a team for five years and start to feel like Superman. But when you get traded, it agitates something within you — makes you angry or upset or motivated — and, if you use that agitation to your advantage, it can push you to the next level. If you use it to prove that you have the capacity to be better than you were before, you're headed toward great.

A setback is a setup for a comeback.

Chris Paul is someone who has always been on the move in the NBA. I think part of what makes him so valuable is that he never gets comfortable in one place. CP3 has never been in a position to become complacent or lazy. No matter where he is — the Hornets to the Rockets to the Clippers to the Suns — the man is just a beast. Let's say he plays 80-some games a season. Of those, he's at his best 60-some times. Most players don't have that dog. They don't have the drive to wake up every day and give 120. I think so much of what makes him who he is relates to his being willing to get uncomfortable, being willing to stretch his muscles and expand his capacity.

When I talk to CP3, I act as a support. He doesn't need me to rebuild his worldview. He needs iron to sharpen iron. On the rare day when he's feeling distracted, I give him a place to focus. If anything, I sometimes put into perspective what it can mean to work with younger teammates or teammates who don't have the same internal drive he does. During times when he's been injured or when he was dealing with Covid during the playoffs in 2021, I reinforce that he's got to control the controllable. As a leader, he can still show up with wisdom. As a teammate, he can still show up as a cheerleader. During the games he was out, Coach Monty Williams FaceTimed him in during halftime, so he could give the guys his love and support.

Once you get comfortable getting uncomfortable and finding satisfaction in the challenge, the way you think begins to shift, too. Your mind is your strongest muscle. And when your mind accepts the challenge, you can start to wake up with that drive. You can begin to see yourself differently, and know that you've got you. Your mind doesn't dream what it cannot achieve. When you decide that you want to be the elite of the elite, you start to act like the elite of the elite—with a fuel that comes from within.

Even Michael Jordan had to figure out a way to progress, to find a way to pull greatness out of himself. He would just make things up— asking other players why they were talking about his mama or why they thought they were better than him, even though they hadn't said anything at all. The most excellent among us always find ways to take their talents to the next level.

The Unfamiliar Is the Most Interesting Place to Be

A couple years ago, I was in Atlanta to speak to a large group of Black entrepreneurs and CEOs. I was doing my pre-talk ritual of meditating and praying in the wings before going on. In my head, I often hear Eminem's lyrics to "Lose Yourself": *The moment you own it you better never let it go / You only get one shot to not miss the chance to blow / This opportunity comes once in a lifetime.* I didn't realize I was being watched by a young kid whose dad was one of the founders of the Circle of CEOs. The boy came up and asked if I was nervous. He couldn't believe it when I said, "Yes, absolutely." He'd seen me on YouTube and was amazed that I still get anxious every time I stand in front of an audience.

But I'm not an entertainer. I'm a coach and a minister. And over the years, I've realized just how high the stakes are when I'm talking to people. The work I'm doing is transformative. People listen to me. I influence them. Every time I speak to an audience, I take it very seriously. And for this reason, I still always get nervous, but it's not something I ever let stop me from doing my thing. I'm so emotional that I have to be careful. If I let them, my emotions could paralyze me. They could stop me from operating in my flow or distract me from the excellence I aim for every day. The difference between the younger E and the E you see today is that I have accepted that my emotions are part of who I am. It's a challenge I embrace. It's a quality that makes me good at what I do.

There is a certain amount of fear built into the notion of sacrificing the familiar for the unfamiliar. But the unfamiliar is the most interesting place to be. When you travel the world, you're purposefully seeking out the unfamiliar. When you learn another language, you're seeking out the unfamiliar. When you read a new book or talk to a new person or watch a new movie, you are seeking out the unfamiliar. And, in doing so, you're cultivating a hunger for knowledge. You could watch the same movie over and over again. You could read the same book a hundred times. And that would be fine. You know it will be good. But if you don't look forward to something new, you'll never know the true meaning of greatness.

Pain produces things that complacency can't.

You cannot let fear stop you from doing what it is you want to do. You cannot let fear keep you in a place of complacency and comfort.

The average human is looking for the comfort zone—the place where things are stable and constant. The average human likes to settle into that feeling, which eventually morphs into the status quo. Good is good, but good doesn't get you the championship. Good is good, but good doesn't get you into the job of president or CEO. Good is good, but it doesn't qualify you for the Olympics. Good is good, but it isn't great. Almost anyone can get something good, but if you want to keep moving forward and level up, you're going to have to come to grips with abandoning good for great.

Leaving the comfort zone can be scary. Discomfort doesn't have to be a bad thing, however. Discomfort is what you feel when you work out and your body is changing. Discomfort is what you feel when you travel to a new country and you don't know where you're going. Discomfort is what builds strength and knowledge and character.

Tea doesn't work unless it's put in hot water. There are some things about us that don't work when we're in a comfort zone. Heat and pressure produce greatness in us. Heat and pressure can be good things if you see them that way. Where your focus goes, your energy flows. If you see fear and discomfort as suffocating, you will be suffocated. But if you identify those feelings with a different way of thinking, you can see what you need to do to become great with new clarity. Sometimes you need the hot water to bring the flavor out of the tea.

But maybe leaving the comfort zone isn't what lies behind your fear. Maybe your fear comes from another place—a place that is concerned with well-being and survival. I know this feeling well. I have always felt the pressure to provide for my family. My motivational speaking career has not always been the bread and butter. I gained lots of other skills and abilities along the way to speaking becoming my main source of income. Today, I am multidimensional. Today, I know that if my voice were to go away, I could continue to provide stability for myself and my family. My fear that I will not be able to provide for them, in this case, is a positive. It keeps challenging me to be well-rounded, to do more and be more than just speaking or teaching or coaching. I think of people like D.O.C.

of N.W.A getting into a car accident and losing his vocals, or Adele losing her voice for two years and having to cancel her tours. I believe that because of where I come from, I am built for survival and part of that means being afraid that I could lose everything. My insurance policy is my excellence, and being excellent at all aspects of what I do in this world.

The World's Vision for You Will Not Always Align with Your Vision for Yourself

For almost five years, working at MSU was smooth sailing. CJ, Karl, and I expanded the Advantage, and we were attracting big audiences, and changing kids' lives at a fundamental level. The Department of Student Affairs was full-on behind every move we made. But things change, and eventually a new director came in and had a different view of how things should be done. Unfortunately, she wasn't as excited about what we were doing at the Advantage as past directors had been. We didn't do things the traditional way, and we were given liberties because we'd changed the entire method of student outreach. These things happen. Just as when a new coach comes in and they want to install their own team, new leaders come in and want things done their way. But the reality was this: The Advantage was a program I didn't get paid to run. It's a program the university didn't fund. And it was a program that drew crowds inside and outside of campus every week. It was making a major difference in the lives of kids of all colors and every socioeconomic status. The Advantage wasn't just good. It was great.

When I recognized that what we were doing wasn't being appreciated, I felt it was time to take my talents elsewhere. Dealing with the tension of the situation was taking energy away from the meaningful work I was attempting to do. The director of the department, Dr. Lee June, didn't want me to leave. He asked me to wait a year and reevaluate. Because concessions were made to bring me in, because so much support was given to me when I arrived at MSU, I was conflicted about leaving outright. So I gave it another year. And at the end of the year, things weren't any better. I had no choice but to leave.

Here's what I found: Leaving that job gave me a freedom I couldn't have had before. Sure, I didn't have benefits or a steady paycheck from MSU, but what I did have was the clarity to understand what I should do next. I found myself freed of distractions, paperwork, and meetings, and I gained a sense of what should come next for me. When you leave a good situation for the promise of great—voluntary or not—you find time to practice your greatness. You gain an understanding of the difference between mediocrity and excellence. You discover what you can keep from your success and what you can leave behind. Just as when a player gets traded, leaving MSU motivated me to push myself to what lay beyond the horizon. I knew greatness was ahead of me. I just had to reach out and take it.

In the end, I kept the Advantage. It still exists and is more popular and diverse than ever. I still speak every Monday evening to anyone who wants to come. We livestream it on Facebook and Instagram, and we have people show up from all over who can't necessarily make it to one of my events. We still don't get paid for the program and the university doesn't fund it, but it's still on campus, and it still lives in the incarnation I'd dreamed of when CJ and I held the very first Monday meetup. We've never compromised on our vision.

Here's the point: Your vision is your vision. You can't let other people hijack your vision or your goals and force their agenda onto your dreams. You have to be cautious about satisfying people's expectations while continuing to honor your own. This is especially true when dealing with large systems—corporations, the government, universities, the NBA, the NCAA. The founders of America had a vision and a dream, but they weren't necessarily the ones who established the infrastructure that actualized the dream. They got Japanese people, Irish people, African people, Hispanic people to build the country they envisioned. People can bully you into fulfilling their dream if you aren't careful. Always keep your own vision within sight.

Greatness Is Not Effortless

When Dede and I arrived at Michigan State, she started attending the Seventh-Day Adventist church in town. At the time, the original pastor had gone overseas, so there was a vacancy for the position. I would volunteer on occasion, and whenever I did the church was filled to capacity with extra seats added to the aisles. Eventually, the membership asked if I would accept a position as lay pastor. I'd finished my master's, I'd gotten hired at Michigan State, and it felt like the right time to make it official. I was ready to settle down. After dragging Dede up North, kicking and screaming, she'd found a great job. The kids were happy. I had two great careers doing everything I loved doing. Life was beautiful.

For four years, working with the church was utopian. When I got there, the congregation was small, but we were able to scale and build in a matter of a year. Eventually, we were at standing-room-only status. But it didn't end there. We were doing good in the community. We organized an after-school youth program. MSU students started coming around to hear me preach. We formed bonds with other congregations and traveled together. We supported members in spiritual and physical crisis. Special speakers and musicians came in to talk and give performances almost every week. We had dinners and barbecues in the park. And the pews were always full. It felt exactly how I imagined life should feel . . . at least for a little while.

I've never gone about anything in the traditional way, including being a pastor. During services, I sat in the front pew instead of at the head of the church. I told stories and gave sermons in the ET way, which is more focused on the human aspect of a message than on doctrine. There's nothing wrong with doctrine. It's just never been my thing. I preach from my experience. The way I saw the change in the church was all positive. To me, people had real needs—emotional, financial, educational needs—and if we could help them on a personal level, we were doing exactly what a church should be doing. It felt like we were in a place of greatness, spreading that greatness into the community.

More and more new members came in—people from all over the community with all kinds of backgrounds. Some old members returned as well. But soon it became clear that some of the more traditional members were having a difficult time adjusting to the shift that was happening in the church. Some people felt I was too modern. Others felt I was too creative in my delivery. Unbeknownst to me, a few of the senior members in leadership had started writing letters to the regional conference officials of the SDA church. Eventually, the president came down to investigate the matter and decided that the church was doing remarkably well. He noted the increase in attendance and participation, but, more important than that, he noted the positive impact on the congregants and the surrounding community.

Unfortunately, this didn't satisfy the traditionalists of the church. They were adamant about maintaining a more conventional and structured approach to their ministry. So, they went over the heads of the regional conference leaders and began to write letters to the officials of the state conference. That group, which is historically motivated by systems, protocols, and traditional methodology, began to put pressure on the regional administration to get rid of me. And it worked. It wasn't long after that letter-writing campaign that I got a call, telling me that I was being relieved of my duties. I was crushed—this was not the ending I wanted—but I was also determined to keep my head high and keep things peaceful. I didn't want to be at odds with anyone at the church. I hate tension. I hate arguing. I loved the people there, and I wanted to do my best with the responsibility that God had given me.

Have you ever been in a place where you were thriving but also stuck? It's strange to think that you could be at the top of your game while simultaneously being so restricted that you couldn't realize your true potential. But this is how things happen sometimes. And sometimes you need a push to get to the next level. In these moments, I find myself inspired by the story of Joseph in the Bible. Like me, Joseph found himself in a paradoxical situation. Banished to prison for a crime he didn't commit, he was still a leader, still finding ways to be the best at his work. There are times when God will send you into environments that are not ideal, but you can still be a blessing. You can still do good work. I took inspiration from Joseph's faith in the midst of his uncertainty and disappointment.

On my final day at the church, in my final sermon, I spoke about Joseph and his faith. When I finished, Dede grabbed my hand, and we, along with Jalin and Jayda, walked toward the doors of the church. And then I did something that, perhaps at the time, many people in the congregation didn't understand: I stopped at the door, untied my shoes, and left them there before walking out of the church. They were a pair of boots that I just loved wearing. They'd been given to me by a member of the congregation as a token of appreciation.

The boots were a symbolic gesture for me for two reasons: First, to me, it felt similar to the end of an engagement or a marriage. A person takes off their ring, and reluctantly places it in their partner's hand before walking away. It's a gesture that the commitment—and all things tied to that commitment—has irrevocably ended. Second, I've learned that you can be in the midst of a dark season and God will begin to shift things in your environment without you even knowing. When he was being released from prison, before Joseph could present himself to the Pharaoh, he was told to shave and change his clothes—to go from a man imprisoned to a man of the world. When you are transitioning from one season to the next, you have to disassociate from those things that are tied to where you're coming from. You have to transition with a clean slate, apart from everything you knew before.

Dede and I were devastated by our loss of the church. We'd given everything we had to building our congregation and giving back to the community. We were in a true place of comfort and peace with the lives we'd built. But when we left behind those deep-burgundy pews, the stained-glass windows, and well-dressed men and women holding their paper fans, we didn't realize the new beginnings we were creating even in the midst of such an emotional ending.

It all makes sense now when I look back on that day. Before my sermon, the choir sang "Praise Him in Advance" by Marvin Sapp. I would never have been able to explain it back then, but even with the devastation my family and I felt, God had already begun preparing a table for us. CJ was sitting in the church at the time. What I didn't realize, but what he later shared with me, was that more than half of the church walked out behind me—dozens of other members were right there behind me and my family as we walked out into the crisp autumn afternoon, the sun and breeze welcoming us into a new season. We walked to our cars with a mix of pain and praise in our hearts.

The next week, I got a call from Dr. Charles Arrington and his wife Simone, who told me they were holding services at their house with all the people who'd walked out. They asked if I'd come and preach in the capacity of pastor whenever I felt ready. I had reservations about it. I didn't want to start any additional trouble with the denomination, but I recalled a verse from the Bible when Jesus asks Peter: "Do you love me?" And Peter answers, "Of course I love you." And Jesus asks again, "Do you love me?" And Peter answers, "Yes, I told you, I love you." And Jesus asks a final time, "Do you love me?" And Peter tells him, "Yes, my lord, I love you." Then Jesus looks at him and says, "If you love me, then feed my sheep." I couldn't deny that there was a flock to lead and people were looking to me as their shepherd.

When I started preaching outside the church, word got out, and the word on the street was that I was blacklisted. I wasn't allowed to attend a church in the Great Lakes conference and I certainly wasn't allowed to speak at any event or church that had any connection to the Seventh-Day Adventist faith. Even Oakwood, my beloved Oakwood, my first home outside of Detroit, wouldn't let me come speak anymore.

This is when I traded up something good for something great. Even though it wasn't my choice, even though I'd been banned from my own faith and my own spiritual home, I couldn't see it as anything but an op-

SACRIFICE GOOD FOR GREAT

portunity to keep moving forward. Even after I spoke at my godparents' church and an official of the faith tried to intimidate me into leaving, I couldn't see anything but a path toward a greater purpose beyond the politics of religion. Nobody has a monopoly on the Bible. Nobody has a monopoly on God. And nobody has a monopoly on faith. Spirituality is so personal. You can't tell people how to practice it. You can just show up for whoever needs it 120.

You must be willing to sacrifice what you are for what you will become.

This was the beginning of the ministry that Dede and I started, called A Place of Change. When we started A Place of Change, we vowed to make it a ministry, rather than a church. We knew it was not going to be a traditional edifice or a traditional system. We knew we wanted to give more to our congregation than they gave to us. We started with fifty or sixty people, holding services all over the place—in homes, in MSU classrooms, in community centers. Eventually, I was able to buy an abandoned medical facility where today, A Place of Change has gathered a community of thousands of people from all over the world. Even during a pandemic, our membership has grown, and we gather every week digitally to practice faith openly. Some weekends, 50,000 people tune in to commune together in prayer. Today, we are in a place of true greatness that we'd never have known if we hadn't been forced to move forward.

This is the beauty of being forced to make sacrifices. Of having to step out into the unknown. Of confronting the fear of discomfort. When you use moments of difficulty and challenge as an opportunity to keep moving forward, you leave yourself open to greatness. Greatness does not come from comfort or ease. Greatness is not effortless. Greatness is built on a defiance of good.

Leaving Good for Great Should Be Emotional

How are you supposed to know when you should leave good for great? How can you recognize the point when you need to trade your current situation for what's to come?

In many cases, you may need to go through a serious emotional experience. Maybe multiple serious emotional experiences. For a lot of us, something has to happen—something tragic, serious, or moving. I didn't just wake up thinking, *Let's go*. I didn't wake up wanting to be great. It took some heavy stuff to agitate the good in me. And then some heavier stuff brought out the great.

In the moment, you may not be able to recognize that what you're being faced with is a moment of leaving good for great. When I left MSU and the church within the same year, my life was upended. Everything changed. In the midst of it all, I couldn't see what was coming next. I didn't know that I was moving from good to great. What I did know was that these experiences were not going to break me, and that the only way to get through them was to move forward. At some point you have to accept what is happening around you. You have to accept the difficulty. And you have to persist.

Once you have acceptance, you can find clarity. You can be intentional about what you want out of the experience. I never go out and run six or seven miles without deciding to ahead of time. With Dede's MS, with the church, with MSU, I decided I would not be broken. I decided I would be elevated by these experiences. Mike Tyson has that famous saying, "Everybody has a plan until they get punched in the mouth." The question is this: Are you going to get up? If you're going to be great, the answer has to be yes. Whatever you go through is worth it on the other side.

Decide how you're going to write the narrative of your journey. When Dede got MS, I asked myself, *What is this going to mean?* We had to decide how it was going to shape us. We decided that we were not going to sit back and wait for it to take its course. We decided to stare it down and give it meaning. The meaning was that we were going to get stronger as a couple, as a family, as a community. We made up our minds that it was going to be the challenge that took our lives to the next level. You can let the world imbue your life with meaning—you can listen to the language and chatter of other people and let it fill you up. Or you can create your own language. You can take the words of your story and your life and fill them up with the meaning and definition you want to give them.

Now watch this: Kobe Bryant said that if you want to be great, you have to be obsessed with it. To go from good to great, you must—I repeat, you *must*—be obsessed with whatever it is you want to be great at. If you want it, you will never settle for good. You will instantly recognize the measure of goodness against greatness and you will intuitively move beyond mere goodness to the level you are reaching for. You have to be willing to let go of predictability and stability. You have to be okay with the feeling of discomfort. You must be like an athlete in the throes of training. You push your mind and your body to their limits to get to the next level of competition. You must have the courage to take yourself beyond average. You owe it to yourself to gather this courage and move toward greatness.

The thing you have to keep sight of in sacrificing good for great is the present moment. Always be where your feet are. The best version of you is actually where your feet are. But if you aren't always developing and growing and changing, you will still be standing in the same place for eternity. Where your feet are will eventually expire.

The Work

1. What in your life right now is good? What is great? What can you observe about the difference between the two?
2. What in your life are you settling for? What are you complacent about? What do you like but not love?
3. Think about the fears that are holding you back. What is stopping you from leaving a job, a relationship, a city, an ideology behind? What are you afraid of losing if you were to leave it behind?

Challenge: Take one of the things in your life that is good. Imagine what it would take for that thing—a job, a relationship, a talent—to move from a place of good into great. What does that process look like and feel like? What does the greatness look like and feel like? What would it feel like to remain in a place of good after having imagined a place of great? What are the emotions surrounding good versus great? What will you lose in moving from one to the other? What will you gain? Compare those things. Imagine moving through the difficulty and the fear. Make a list of steps for how you might begin to move this good thing or situation into a place of greatness.

You Are a Business

ANYBODY CAN BE A BUSINESSPERSON WHEN YOU START WITH WHAT YOU HAVE.

Nobody talks about the business of Malcolm X or Martin Luther King Jr. Nobody tells you how Marcus Garvey or Huey Newton paid their bills or who handled their finances. I don't think Sojourner Truth or Frederick Douglass were getting a payout after they spoke at a rally. When I started doing motivational speaking for a living, there was no how-to guide that I could refer to for advice on becoming the world's best motivational speaker. The world of motivational speaking is rarefied, and one that, when I was coming up, was not populated with many people who looked or sounded like me. As I got deeper into the speaking circuit, I operated out of instinct and impulse for the most part. I naturally moved toward the spirit of ministry and service. The word *strategy* wasn't even in my vocabulary in regard to building a business until a few years ago.

For many years, I didn't realize the monetary value of my voice. I could see that the way I spoke affected people and moved crowds. I could see that I had the ability to bring forth emotion and provoke thought. But I couldn't see the breadth or range of opportunities that my voice and my set of abilities presented in terms of financial gain. If you can believe it, there was a point when I didn't know that I had a business built right into my body. When people started requesting my presence as a speaker, I was just grateful for the opportunity. When people started to pay me for speaking gigs, I was excited about it, but I didn't think of it as a way to make a living. It had never occurred to me that I could get paid for something that was so inextricable from my own existence.

When CJ and I came together at Michigan State, it was obvious that

217

he had an inherent sense of how to do business. He has never been afraid to ask for resources or make decisions or execute a job. While I was always about interacting and being with the people, CJ has always been thinking up new ways to present our material or scale our programming. By 2005, we had the Advantage up and running, but beyond that we didn't necessarily know what came next. We just kept building a following, advising our kids, and working in the community.

At some point, Karl showed up. He was a quiet guy who started coming around the Advantage in the beginning and never left. Born in Barbados and educated in biology and media, Karl is one of those people who will do any odd job, figure out how anything technological works, and do it more meticulously and obsessively than anyone else without expecting anything in return. Eventually, he'd been around for so long, volunteering and pitching in, that he just became part of the crew. When CJ, Karl, and I became a team, we didn't have a grand plan, but we had a feeling that together we could make something big happen.

Today, we like to describe our roles this way: I am the voice, CJ is the brain, and Karl is the hands. In terms of the Flight Assessment, I am a Flight Attendant. I like to be around new people and work from my emotions and impulse. CJ is a Pilot, meaning he is a decision maker and a power broker. He works from a place of logic. Karl is a Grounds Crew, which means he's a supporter, offering consistency and predictability. He's at his best when he is given direction and structure and can work with expectations and benchmarks. We didn't realize it when we got together, but we were excellently suited for one another when it came to running a business. Because we all have different skill sets and personality traits, when we communicate effectively, we run like a well-oiled machine. But this realization didn't come until later, so we worked through a lot with plain old trial and error.

When CJ surveyed the field of professional speakers, he saw that there were dozens of people who were financially successful. He realized that we had the potential not only to get serious about motivational speaking as a real professional career path, but to make money doing it. CJ knew I was good, but the problem he identified was that nobody knew who I was. You can be amazing at your job, but if nobody knows who you are or where to find you, you're not going anywhere. CJ knew that in America, celebrities walk on water. When you're a celebrity, you walk in places and people see you. We were walking in places and nobody knew us from Adam.

One of the first lessons I learned in business is that you must state what you are and where you're going so that the world can perceive you the way you want to be perceived. Before anyone else perceives you in that role, you have to be willing to envision yourself in that role. I have always called myself a "community activist" and a "motivational speaker." In order for the rest of the world to see me this way, I had to say it myself. I had to invoke and internalize my own vision. You must look at yourself in the mirror and say: I am an artist. I am a doctor. I am an entrepreneur. I am a motivational speaker. Of course, there may be degrees and education between you and the actual undertaking of that role in some cases, but if you can begin to envision yourself in the role and say to yourself that you have what it takes to embody that role, then you can begin to move toward it.

Start Where You Are with What You Have

Once you state your intentions, you can begin to see more clearly the opportunities in the world that align with those intentions.

As soon as CJ, Karl, and I put our efforts as a group toward a singular focus, we could see things starting to happen. One booking led to another and another. Eventually, the guru video hit. And then Thomas Davis called from the Panthers. He'd been watching my videos for years and thought I might bring some inspiration to the team. Kaleb Thornhill, in the Miami Dolphins' player development department, called. Stephen Tulloch, who was a linebacker at the Detroit Lions, called. He'd been watching my videos since college. And from the NBA, Lawrence Frank, who was coaching at the Pistons, called.

Though we'd been working and grinding for years, when success arrived, it felt like a crazy wave rushing at us. Suddenly, we were drowning in opportunities.

The funny thing is, we didn't have a plan beyond me blowing up. We didn't know what success would look like so we didn't know how to prepare for it. So we just made it all up as we went along. When people started calling to book us, they'd tell CJ to "send over the contract." But we'd never dealt with a contract. So CJ called LaShanna Fountain, a woman from my church who was in law school at the time, and she helped us get our official documents together. We didn't have a website and we didn't know how to build one, so when a fan of ours, a kid by the name of Courtney Ray, called and volunteered to build a site for free, we took him up on it. We didn't have a logo, so one morning, CJ drew it on the back of his business card while sitting in his car waiting for a meeting to start.

Every time something new came our way, we just sat down and learned how to do it. Business can be complicated. But it can also be simple. Start where you are with what you have. And what you have is plenty. Martin Luther King Jr. said, "You don't have to see the whole staircase, just take the first step." This is a lesson for life and for business. One step will lead to another step. You don't have to start out with all the latest tech wizardry. You don't need to have a big budget. In the beginning, look at what you have access to and use that. After you take care of that next step, whatever is next will come.

A major part of what has made us successful is our scrappy, grind mentality. We have always been about getting the job done, even if it's with duct tape and glue. Before we started working on this book, we didn't have any connections to the publishing world or any real idea of how to make a book, but we knew that every other motivational speaker had a book out. So we wrote our own books, and then we published them ourselves. On the first run, we had all the books sent to my house in Lansing. On the day of delivery, an eighteen-wheeler truck drove into my neighborhood and dropped off thousands and thousands of copies. My garage was so full of books, Dede couldn't put the car in anymore. Every day, we sat down and I'd sign hundreds of them while CJ and Karl packaged them up and shipped them at USPS flat rate. When we went to events, I'd put them in the back of my car and sell them right out of my trunk. We sold over 300,000 copies that way.

This kind of throw-it-together process won't work forever, but in the beginning, entrepreneurship is about trial and error. It's about figuring out what the job is and getting it done. It's about putting yourself in miracle territory over and over again to see what kinds of opportunities are out there. Being successful in business has a lot to do with a willingness to learn on the job, to experiment, and to try again when the experiment fails. But when the experiment succeeds, you can look at it as a model for growth.

The guru video was an experiment, and it took a few years to understand its payoff, but once we did, we had a blueprint for how to move forward. After that video blew up, CJ realized that we needed another hit. No recording artist wants to be a one-hit wonder, so CJ started deconstructing what was so successful about my messages. We'd been recording my presentations for several years by this point, so he would sift through them, and find my most impactful material. From there, he would tell Karl how to cut and edit a video, Karl would do it, put it up on YouTube, and release it to the world. Between us and our media team, we've experimented with Facebook, Instagram, Snapchat, TikTok, and every other digital platform that's come along since. Sometimes it works, sometimes it doesn't. But it's always worth trying, because experimentation is miracle territory after all.

Hang with People in Business

While CJ was working on getting my name out there, Karl and I were doing our thing at Michigan State. CJ's wife Candis had a job in upstate New York, so he was out there grinding on his own behind the scenes. To be honest, I still really wasn't in a business state of mind. I was grinding, but I wasn't necessarily focused on making money or learning the ins and outs of creating and running systems. I was getting plenty of speaking gigs, but I still wasn't operating with a real strategy. Up until then, the level of our grind made up for the fact that we didn't have a real plan for the future. However, when I started working with Dan Gilbert and Bill Emerson the scales fell from my eyes.

After my boy Tony helped me through corporate training, he introduced me to Dan and Bill and they brought me into the fold almost immediately. They offered me an office right across from theirs. I think it had something to do with the Michigan State connection and the Detroit connection, but also because they saw something in me that they thought was worth investing in. I believe they saw my excellence and wanted to help me reach the next level. They recognized that I had a gift and felt compelled to help me build on it.

This was in 2012. At that time, downtown Detroit was still pretty dead. A few new things had started to crop up, but, for the most part, it felt like a ghost town. Dan and Bill were in the process of buying property all over the city through their real estate company, Bedrock. Their building on Woodward was right in the heart of the city and it was massive. The first time Karl and I walked in, we were like little kids, mouths open, staring at everything. It was like an alien world. Everybody was dressed the same, everybody looked the same, everybody talked the same. It seemed like every person in that place was drinking some kind of Kool-Aid. In every room, there was a colorful wall painted with the company's "isms," or the beliefs and missions that they were focusing on that year. They had a literal playbook published annually that outlined what the new isms were and how they were going to be accomplished. There was a graphics team, a media team, a marketing team, and a team of people who seemed to just sit around and come up with ideas.

I'll never forget, one day somebody pulled me and Karl into a meeting so we could hear about an idea they were conceptualizing. A bunch of people were all hanging around talking about creating a stock exchange for shoes—a place where people could go online and buy and sell shoes the way you might buy and sell shares of Tesla or a piece of art at an auction. Karl and I thought they were nuts. I wear Jordans. I'm not ignorant about the culture of gym shoes. But I also thought that kids from the projects weren't gonna get online and start trading shoes. They'd go down to the store like everybody else, get their ticket, and stand in line for the drop. That night, Karl and I drove home shaking our heads, thinking these guys had lost their minds.

That meeting was where the online marketplace StockX was conceived; it has since been valued at $1 billion. That's what it was like hanging around a real business every day.

Sitting in Dan and Bill's office was like business boot camp—everything from learning the lingo to seeing how meetings went down to understanding how people interact in a corporate environment. I used to think that they were just about Quicken Loans and owning the Cleveland Cavaliers. But they have their hands in dozens of different fields. At the time, they had thirty-some businesses—banking, sports, real estate, mortgages. Dan Gilbert is the only person I ever met who had three executive assistants. There were days when I saw Warren Buffett coming through the office, where I sat in meetings with top members of the team. Kyrie Irving came through. Chauncey Billups came through. Mark Jackson, you name it. And we were so new to the game, we would just sit around and ask them all questions, soaking up the knowledge.

One of the most valuable lessons I learned in gaining a glimpse into this world was that there was nobody Black at the top level. I learned that we had much work ahead of us to put ourselves in places where decisions were being made. While I didn't see myself in those rooms, I knew I had to get us into them. Instead of growing frustrated, I became excited about the prospect of changing this paradigm. Getting into the room gave me another level of confidence and belief. I got into the room because I was doing the work I set out to do.

What Karl and I had was an à la carte opportunity to take whatever subject we wanted on any given day and just learn about it. Neither of us was familiar with the language of business. I have passion and the ability to tell stories, but I didn't have the kind of language and vocabulary that Tony Robbins and Zig Ziglar had. First of all, I didn't grow up in white culture, and second of all I didn't go to business school. The marketing acronyms alone were a new thing for me. Sitting around in that big office, we started to pick up on the cultural cues and codes that have become second nature to businesspeople. We had access to every resource we could imagine—editors, writers, an art department, media connections. We got tickets to NBA games, sitting right behind LeBron during the playoffs. It was like we had backstage passes 24/7. The kind of experience we had working with Dan and Bill opened our eyes to what was possible if we started to put together a strategy and a team.

Meanwhile, we'd hired LaShanna, the law student who helped us early on in the game, once she graduated law school and had done some time working for BET in DC. An Atlanta native, she filled in a lot of the gaps that we just hadn't thought of business-wise. She pulled together legal operations, HR needs, and helped us strategize what our business could look like. Today, she operates as our COO. And while she was figuring out logistics, CJ was undergoing his own lessons about how to do business. Karl and I could soak up vocabulary and ideas, but CJ knew that if we were going to make money and run a proper business, we needed to be more focused and strategic about how we were creating and putting work out into the world.

He started to study other motivational speakers' businesses and realized that they almost always operated on a pay-to-play model. If you go to a speaker's website, you get a little bit of something free—a few minutes of content, a snippet of a message, the beginning of a step-by-step plan—and then, when you're hooked, you have to pay to keep going. Our business wasn't built like that. Because we started off in the digital age, we've always been competing with a sea of free content. We have always given content away, not only in the spirit of ministry, but because we were trying to attract an audience. Many established speakers already had a built-in audience, so they could afford to require people to pay.

CJ doesn't formulate business strategy in the sense of P&Ls and traditional forecasting—LaShanna took on that role. Instead, he has a deep intuition for marketing and branding, and he knew that if he could get my name out into the world, we'd be able to generate revenue and figure out the rest as we went along. He knew that instead of trying to go out to Fortune 500 companies and corporate businesses, if we focused our energy on creating our own content, and putting it out into the world, eventually those companies would come to us. Once the phone started ringing, we began to hold our own events and listen to what our supporters needed from us.

For all of us, undertaking an education in what makes our business tick and how money is made in our particular field was a necessary step to reaching the next level. To sustain our lives, our families, the business itself, we needed to soak in the knowledge of how business is conducted. In some fields, you need a real education. You can't just show up to a hospital to be a nurse or a doctor—you have to get intimate with the field before you're permitted to participate in it. In my field, however, you actually can just show up and be a motivational speaker. Not necessarily at the same level, but you can talk and people somewhere will listen. Likewise, anyone can start a business. Anyone can go to the Chamber of Commerce and fill out paperwork. But over 50 percent of businesses fail because their owners haven't spent the time getting to know what they need to do. They haven't studied the industry they're a part of. They aren't obsessed with their craft and their field.

> **Don't think about what can happen in a month or a year. Focus on the 24 hours in front of you, and do what you can do to get closer to where you want to be.**

Start by figuring out what you're going to do and what you need to get it done. For a basketball team, the coach knows what they need before they even start practice. You need twelve players. You need a point guard, a shooting guard, a power forward, a small forward, and a center. Then you need to know if you're an offensive or a defensive team. Based on that model, you figure out what you need to do to make your team and your strategy work.

In my field, we knew we wanted to equip and empower the everyday person with the energy they needed to make it through the day. And we knew we needed a way to distribute that knowledge, which means we needed people who know how to navigate social media. We needed people who are good at filming and producing. We needed people who are tech-savvy to bring these worlds together.

But, of course, knowledge is simply not enough to run a business. You need people who can get a job done. You need people who can execute. This is where the Flight Assessment comes in handy. The best teams have an array of personality types—the Pilot to drive the operation, the Air Traffic Controller to guide the team's progress, the Flight Attendant to make sure the relationships are running smoothly, and the Grounds Crew to provide support.

How do you attract the right team? This is partly about operating in excellence. Nobody wanted to play for the Cavs back in the '90s. But then LeBron showed up. Not everyone wanted to play for Golden State, but then the Splash Brothers showed up. When you execute at an excellent level, people want to start working for you. Nearly every good idea started with one person who was passionate about making it real. Passion is attractive and it brings people to your side.

Attracting the right people is also about surrounding yourself with people who are successful at what they do. No matter what field they're in, people who are passionate and profitable in their professional lives will have lessons to share with you. Just by being in a new environment with new people, you'll hear new modes of thought, new words, and new perspectives on life and work. Even if they don't apply to your particular interest, knowing how other people think—both here and in other parts of the world—is valuable in shaping your own way of thinking and your own way of doing business. Look at who the most successful people in the world hang out with—other successful people. Artist salons and think tanks and professional societies exist for a reason—for people in those fields to share knowledge and new ideas. Do a deep dive into your particular field. Find out where its most successful people are hanging out and what they're studying. Go to a conference or a talk or read a book by a leader in the field. Surround yourself with the material and people you want to learn from and emulate.

Know Your Literal Worth

When I started making money from speaking engagements, I wasn't sure how to process the meaning of it. I was just pumped to have the opportunity and any kind of compensation. I didn't think too much about my rates because I was so grateful that I had a rate at all. I took what I was given. If MSU paid me $800 to come talk, my rate was $800. If they upped it to $1,500, my rate was $1,500. That I was even getting paid to speak was a major shift from years spent at church and at schools as a minister and counselor. But an encounter with the self-help author and motivational speaker Bob Proctor changed how I thought about myself and my literal worth.

In 2012, I started doing work with Verve, a marketing company. My contract with them was sweet. I would do fourteen gigs a year for them for $140,000. Not only would they hand me a check for $140K, but they would fly me and my family first class, put us up in a hotel suite, and pay for my expenses while I was working. If we were near the water, we had an oceanfront room. If we were in a city, we could see the skyline. A Cadillac would come pick us up, and when we got into our rooms, there was always some nice gift waiting for us. I had never experienced that kind of luxury before. Compared to everything else I'd experienced up to that point, I thought I had made it.

At one of these gigs I was standing backstage when Bob Proctor came up to me. He asked me straight-up, "How much do you charge?" I told him I let the companies tell me what to charge. He said he wouldn't recommend that, and proceeded to tell me that he would charge $20,000 an engagement. Or at least that's what I thought I heard. I was stunned.

Where I'm from, nobody makes that kind of money. My parents probably made $70K or $80K toward the end of their careers. To think I could get that kind of money for four speaking gigs sounded crazy. Even my doctor and lawyer friends weren't getting paid that kind of money. When companies called, and CJ told them our new rate, we started getting it. I was flabbergasted that the companies were willing to pay me that kind of money. A part of me thought that because Bob Proctor was white, he could get away with it, but, sure enough, when I asked for it, I got it, too.

Three or four months later, I ran into Bob again at a conference, and he pulled me to the side and asked me how my work was coming. I thanked him for his advice, and told him I had taken his recommendation of asking for $20,000 a gig. He said, "I never told you to charge $20,000. I said you should charge no less than $20,000." I had gotten so focused on the number that I hadn't heard what he was really saying. And what he was really saying is that there was no ceiling. My mind was blown. I had never had anyone volunteer that kind of information before. It opened up a whole new world for me.

This is how you become a magnet for greatness. When you start behaving like, talking like, looking like greatness—once you get it into your brain that you want to be great—you start attracting greatness. You start getting into environments where Bob Proctor comes up and talks to you. When your obsession with greatness is real—when it's not a facade and when it's not about extrinsic desires—you find people who share your common mind-set and your work ethic. You attract what you are. It takes greatness to attract greatness.

Success is never on discount. Greatness is never on sale. Greatness is never half off.

The way I saw my worth before was from a place of gratitude. I was just happy to be in the room. It's not that I wasn't aware that white men in the same field with less talent than me were earning more—I was always aware of that—I just knew that I wasn't in a position to say no to any kind of rate. There's a pecking order in America. And Black men aren't the ones writing the checks in the corporate world. Even when I started working with the NFL, players were paying me out of their own pockets to come speak to their teams. I knew that I was doing for free what white men were doing for fat paydays. But I also knew that getting into those locker rooms and locking gigs with the league—no matter who was writing the check—would pay off in its own way. In the end, I got credibility and I got what I am worth.

Your worth is often built into your difference. In my case, I walk into a room and the people in that room relate to me because we are from the same place. A white speaker in a suit can't go into locker rooms and talk to the guys I talk to and have the same resonance. A corporate coach can't go into the schools I go into and grab the attention of the kids I speak to. I grew up in the same neighborhoods and attended the same schools as those players and those kids. I grew up with my city affected by gang violence. I have uncles and cousins in prison. I grew up without my biological father. I know what that life is about. Life ain't been no crystal stair, as Langston Hughes would say. To a lot of my audience, I look familiar and I sound familiar, and, even if I don't, we have something in common—we are vulnerable humans who have had hard times. And people who have had hard times—we know each other when we see each other. I see you. You see me.

To keep progressing, it's necessary to constantly reevaluate your skill set and skill level against your worth. If you don't value yourself, nobody else is going to value you, either. Get informed on what the rates of your industry are. Understand what it takes to get to each rate and then surpass it. Hold yourself to a standard and evaluate if you're reaching that standard. Once you know your value, ask for it. If you know your value isn't being met, weigh the unmet value against the benefits and costs of the job. If the benefits—say, connections, incentives, opportunities for growth—outweigh the costs, perhaps the lost monetary value can be made up for in the experience of the job itself. If the costs outweigh those benefits, remain firm in the belief of your value.

Of course, not every opportunity can be based on money alone. Sometimes opportunities come with intangible value. When I got my first gig with Quicken Loans, it was far below my rate because I was hired not by the company itself but by an employee who was passionate about having me come speak. Knowing it was a way to get my foot in the door, I took the gig. I've done a lot of work for free to get where I am, and I still do free work almost every day. This is the kind of stuff that builds value and keeps me in the habit of practicing my purpose. I don't wake up every day to get paid. I wake up every day to walk in my purpose.

You won't be successful until I don't have to give you a dime to do what you do.

Keep Perspective

After I started to get known in the NBA and the NFL, I began getting calls from celebrities. P. Diddy, Tyrese Gibson, Reggie Bush—they were all calling me at Michigan State. That's when you know you've made it—when P. Diddy is calling your office line at the university. I got offers to hit the movie set, to fly out on the private plane and chill in Cali, but I've never been about that life. I've always believed that I needed to stay focused on my own grind. Of course, I'm super flattered when I receive the invitation, and it gets me pumped and makes me feel validated, but I don't need to be spending my downtime with multimillionaires who have already made it. I'm trying to make it. I don't need to see what that life looks like because I'm trying to make my own life.

When you start to become successful financially, you have to keep perspective. If you've done the work up front—listening to your inner-most self, staying authentic to your why, consistently evaluating your progress, your purpose, and nurturing your power—your success should only be a blessing. Wealth can be complicated, especially if you don't know yourself or haven't taken the time to really understand your why and your purpose and what it is you want beyond money.

So many of the athletes I work with are hit with massive paydays at the beginning of their careers. All of a sudden they've got more money than they know what to do with, lights shining in their faces, and media keeping tabs on their fashion, their tweets, their social lives. Most of these guys are kids just coming into their adult minds and emotions. The average adolescent has a difficult time coping with this transition, but add money and fame to it? Perspective isn't easy.

When you grow up an athlete, the focus is singular: making it to the league. But once many athletes make it to the league, there's little guidance on how to manage wealth and fame. Making it to any league means considering yourself a business. It means finding balance within the success to maintain the success. For my guys in the league, I give them this perspective: You have an expiration date. You're eighteen, nineteen, twenty, twenty-one years old, and your career will likely max out before the age of thirty-five. Then I ask them: What does your life look like after the league?

Life after Success Requires Thinking like a Businessperson

When you experience success, the journey does not end there. Arguably, you must work to protect what you've achieved with even more strategy than you began with. Ironically, life after success can be difficult. When you've achieved what you set out to do, how do you continue to progress?

First, and most important, you must remember why you started working toward your success in the first place. This means refocusing on your purpose and your why. Just because you rise to a certain level does not mean your purpose disappears or your why goes away. These continue to be the fuel behind your continued progress. You cannot let success distract you from your purpose or your why. You cannot let the trappings of success take away from your focus.

For me, success is not only about money and stability and validation. Success is about self-actualization. When I coach successful athletes or CEOs, I point to Abraham Maslow's hierarchy of needs. The hierarchy puts physiological needs—shelter, food, etc.—at the bottom. Safety needs are above that, then come love and belonging, next is esteem, and finally, at the top, is self-actualization. In reality, most athletes have secured the bottom two tiers of the pyramid. Though sports are valued in society and being a professional athlete is equal to celebrity status, most athletes are dealing with the same struggles as people who have normal jobs—time management, feeling accepted and loved, gaining confidence. The two main issues with athletes is that money has the ability to create a facade of stability. It can create the mirage of actualization. The singular focus of making it to the league and then staying in the league as long as possible can distract them from moving up the hierarchy of needs toward cerebral functions.

When time in the league is up, the break between the psyche and the established reality becomes visible. There are endless stories of players leaving professional sports and feeling lost without the structure of a schedule or the singular focus of keeping their bodies in prime physical shape. Drugs, debt, and divorces all form a common thread in these stories. This isn't uncommon for those who have made it to the equivalent of their "league," no matter what the profession. Once they reach the top tier of success and wealth, perspective and purpose can become threatened if self-actualization hasn't been reached.

One of my favorite examples about self-actualization is my friend Jemal King. Today, Jemal goes by the name "the 9 to 5 Millionaire." Jemal is from Chicago and grew up in the 1980s as a very gifted athlete. He got scouted for the NFL, but in his junior year of college at Western Illinois, he suffered a career-ending injury. Jemal turned to the next most logical profession: He became a police officer. The CPD was in his blood. His mother, father, and siblings were or are all in law enforcement in Chicago. Seeing his friends get drafted by the NFL was difficult, but he knew he wasn't going to get left behind. For years, Jemal was in that grind. He and his wife saved their money and eventually bought a little bit of real estate. And then they bought some more. Jemal became a millionaire while working a full-time job with the Chicago Police Department. But after achieving monetary success and stability, he didn't stop there. Eventually, he opened day-care centers for the neighborhoods he was working in. Then he began coaching students in the surrounding schools to teach them the basics of real estate so they could buy back their own blocks and take care of their own neighborhoods. Today, Jemal lives on Millionaire's Row in Chicago, a place where men who looked like him wouldn't have dreamed of living a century ago. Today, he's not only successful but actualized. He has a why. He has a path of purpose.

Today, we can look at the model set by so many athletes whose physical careers are temporary. People like LeBron James, Dwyane Wade, Chris Paul—these guys have led careers that will land them in the category of greatest of all time, but they haven't let their athletic ability be the sole factor in their development as humans.

Even in your moments of great success, you must return to your why. These are the moments where centering yourself in purpose will keep you moving toward the parts of yourself that are real and true. If you're listening to the outside world—the fans, the media, the naysayers—you won't be able to hear yourself or see your path of purpose.

Learn from Your Forebears

By 2012, I was consistently getting gigs with NFL teams. More and more corporations were getting in touch, and I seemed to be in miracle territory all the time. And then I got a call from Les Brown.

In the speaking world, Les Brown is a legend. In my community he's the GOAT. The first African American to really make it in the modern motivational-speaking world, Les is respected as a business and professional guru. Les and his twin brother were born in an abandoned building in Liberty City, Miami. He was adopted by a woman named Mamie Brown who worked for white families as a housekeeper, bringing home leftover food and hand-me-down clothes. Les was declared "educable mentally retarded" in the fifth grade and sent back to the fourth grade. I never had it as bad as Les, but I could relate to his story and I felt close to him without even knowing him.

When he called, I remember thinking, *Okay, this is it, let's go.* When Les said he wanted to connect, I was in Orlando three days later with Karl. We acted like we had business in the area, and got a nice hotel room for the day, even though we were only there for eight hours or so. Waiting for Les to arrive felt like being dressed up for the prom, waiting for your date at the door. We were nervous. When he got there, he looked just like Les Brown. You never know after you see somebody on TV or in photos if that's the real deal, but there he was in the flesh. He walked in, gave us both a hug, and was ready to work. I interviewed him for about thirty minutes on camera. We talked about finding a why—his was taking care of his mother and making her proud—figuring out what you want to do, telling the world, and then waking up every day and going after it. Talking to Les was a dream fulfilled.

When the camera was off, Les turned to me and told me he had some words of advice. Very candidly, he told me I had what it took to be the best in the world, but that there were things I could work on to get to that next level.

First, he told me that I needed to value my difference. He said that comparison is the thief of happiness and joy. Les assured me that my experience as a Black man in America was going to take me to a different level, not just because there were Black people in business who needed to hear my story, but because our history and our culture and our world-view were all relevant to so many people's struggles. People needed to hear about my own journey to success to know that they could get there, too. Les reassured me that, just as there are advantages to being a left-handed pitcher in a right-handed game, there were advantages to being a Black man in a white business. He told me I could relax into those advantages and enjoy them.

Second, Les told me I needed to value myself financially. He asked me what I was charging and I told him. Even after my lesson from Bob Proctor, Les told me I was still undervaluing myself. "You should be charging $50K nationally and $100K internationally," he said. My jaw dropped. He promised me that it was fair, and that because I brought something entirely unique to the industry I was more valuable than I was probably aware of. But he also reinforced the idea behind it: Nobody is going to value me if I don't value myself. It's up to me to tell people what I'm worth.

I let all of that sink in. That day, I felt that Les was cosigning me. Les is the OG, and I found myself that day in the position of receiving the torch from the man who'd gone further than anyone else in our community. To hear him affirm my work and validate me on a level no one else in the world could understand gave me the fire I needed to go after it.

I went back to work.

Embrace Being an Outsider

Early on, when I started getting deep into personal development books, and knew I wanted to be in the motivational-speaking industry, I surveyed who was big in the field—past and present. Back then, it was Earl Nightingale, Zig Ziglar, Brian Tracy, Wayne Dyer, Bob Proctor, Jim Rohn, Stephen Covey, and Les Brown. Every single one of those people, except for Les, is a white male. Looking at it from the outside, breaking into that industry seemed like an insurmountable task.

As I was growing and developing my speaking skills, hip-hop was growing and developing, too. When I got to Oakwood in '89, hip-hop was taking root in a major way. It may not have been mainstream, as it is today, but in the Black community it was everything. Hip-hop was telling the story of our culture in a way it had never been told before. It was giving the world another perspective beyond the white experience. Around the same time, Black television was starting to take off as well. When I watched TV growing up, it was predominantly white characters living in white cultures. When the Cosbys came on and then Fresh Prince and then Martin, it was obvious there was a hunger for another way of seeing the world.

Seeing all this, and seeing how one-dimensional the motivational-speaking world was, I knew there was a space for me in it. Most speakers at that time were talking on a corporate level to people interested in business. Nobody was talking about personal and professional development on a street level. The way I saw it, the business sector is large, with a huge, untapped audience. White corporate speakers aren't going to go to the East Side of Detroit or the West and South Side of Chicago. They aren't going to Gary, Indiana, or Huntsville, Alabama. They're not hitting juvenile detention centers or urban schools. My people weren't being exposed to that kind of thinking, so I saw the opportunity to do it in a way no one else had, up to that point.

When you're trying to figure out where you fit in to your field, first look at how you don't fit. When I talked to Les Brown, I saw that the very reason I didn't fit in was how I could distinguish myself. When you compare yourself to everyone else in your field, use that exercise to discover where the gaps are. What does your field lack and how can you step into that space and fill it? You may need to spend some time with yourself and figure out what that means. Stop listening to everybody else and listen to yourself. You may need to go within and get quiet to hear what it is you want to say. You may need to block out other voices so that you can get to know your own voice. Once you know your difference, you can lean in to it and bring that to the forefront of your own work.

Your difference is always what makes you valuable—not only theoretically valuable, but literally valuable. And once you know your difference, it is your responsibility to get every single dime of your worth. If you want to get what you're worth, you have to speak up. You have to get organized and present yourself in a way that reflects your worth. This doesn't necessarily mean how you dress—I can tell you firsthand that this has nothing to do with it—but it means everything when it comes to how you conduct business.

Of course, it can be scary to look inward. To acknowledge your difference. To feel like you don't belong. It can also be scary to confront your value and ask what you need to do to become more valuable, to become more excellent. But, I promise you, it will bring you in to a new sense of yourself. When I did this work on my own, when I looked inward, I saw what I brought to the table: I bring energy. I bring transparency. I bring reflection. I am not afraid to talk about my own vulnerabilities and challenges. I am not afraid to tell the world about where I'm from. I come from a place of seeking healing before I could reach a place of seeking wealth. Yes, you might have to face the fear of being an outsider or the fear of not being accepted. That's not a race thing. That's a human thing. We all want to be affirmed. We all want to be valued. We all want to be a part of a community. But you can't allow your fear to hold you back from being your authentic self. You can't let your fear keep you from doing what it is that you're meant to do. You have to be willing to take a risk to be great.

You Owe It to Yourself to Be Exactly Who You Are

Back in 2009, after talking with Bob Proctor about what I should be getting paid, I wasn't feeling that I could ask for $20,000 just yet, but I challenged CJ to start asking for a higher rate. The first time he asked for $10K, it was from a corporate company that inquired to see if I was available to speak at a formal event. After CJ told them the rate, the booker said she'd confirm it with her company. The next day she called CJ back and said my $10,000 rate was approved. The only catch was that the CEO wanted to make sure I would wear a suit for the occasion. I'll never forget CJ calling me and telling me we were good to go; all I had to do was wear a suit.

I remember saying flat out: "A suit? I'm not wearing no suit." I have to admit, I was a little bit shocked that C would entertain the idea. I told C he had to call the booker back and tell her I couldn't do it. CJ pushed me on it. He felt like the gig was a win, especially because we'd been trying to do corporate for so long and were finally getting in and getting with the rates we were asking for. Also, at the time, we were doing well, but we weren't by any means well off. The company was good, but we weren't necessarily in a position to be turning down ten Gs. But I was holding firm. I told him to relay the message: "If I have to wear a suit, I can't do it." He waited for a couple days, and called me again to see if I had changed my mind.

I put it to him straight. I said, "Yo, C, this is the brand we built. It's the hat and the T-shirt and the gym shoes. This is how we represent in the world, and I can't just start changing that around for money. This is me." I felt I had paid my dues. I'd been in the game for twenty years at that point. I'd been playing by the rules for so long that I didn't want to compromise anymore. There are things I'm willing to compromise on — the time, the place, the content of a presentation — but my appearance is not one of them. I felt like, growing up in this country, my people have been compromising for so long. We've done the A, B, and C that the system asked us to do, and we still can't collect the reward? Now they want us to do D, E, and F? I was just tired of tap-dancing. The truth is, if a suit and tie are so important to you, philosophically speaking, I am not the speaker for you. You're focusing on decorum and I'm focusing on development.

To be fair, I understood where CJ was coming from. He was in his twenties and not as far down the road less traveled as I was. When I talk about it with him today, he admits that he was hurt and frustrated and thought I was crazy. But I knew that I had to be true to the thing that is most me. I owed it to myself to be authentic. He thought we were coming out ahead on the money front, but when I explained it to him my way, he understood.

CJ called the booker back and told her that the hat and gym shoes were non-negotiable. She was shocked that we were going to turn down ten grand for an outfit change. I felt the same way: You're going to turn me down for an outfit change?

A few months later, CJ got a call from another corporate company.

He told the booker the rate—which at that point was even higher than $10K—and she said she'd go back to the company to see if she could get it approved. The next day, she called CJ back and said we were good to go, but there was one thing she needed to be clear about. CJ just had a feeling she was going to ask about my hat and gym shoes, so he prepared himself for the conversation. The woman on the other end of the line said, "We just want to make sure: Can he wear his hat and his gym shoes? It's how we know him from all his videos."

Free at last, free at last. I cannot tell you how good that triumph felt. Where, at first, my dedication to my own truest self was a liability, eventually it became an asset. Now people don't expect me to show up at a corporate gig with khakis and a blue button-down shirt and penny loafers just because that's what the people in the office wear. They don't expect me to show up at a school wearing a uniform because that's what the students wear. NFL players don't expect me to show up in their locker room with a jersey and pads on because that's what they wear. They ask me to come in to speak because I am not them. They ask me to come in and speak because I am me.

Yeah, it might just seem like a T-shirt and shoes, but there is a method to my madness. I am comfortable when I dress like me. I feel good when I dress like me. I feel like me when I dress like me. This is what I wear to church and to parties. It's what I wear to holidays and graduations. If I just go changing what makes me feel good and most in my own skin for any amount of money, what does that say about me? It says I'm willing to shift who I am. I owe it to myself to be the most me I can be.

The world will try to bully you into conforming. The world will try to make you feel that you should follow a certain ideology or assimilate into the mainstream. But you owe it to yourself to stay true to you. You are the most powerful when you are you. I am the most powerful when I am me. You owe it to yourself to be you. I owe it to myself to be me.

I am called ET, the hip-hop preacher, because of where I'm from. How I grew up. The experiences I went through. All of that shaped me and makes me different from everybody else. I grew up listening to hip-hop, took my fashion cues from LL Cool J, Run DMC, UTFO, the Fat Boys. I was wearing the hats, the jogging suits, the jeans. That's why I dress the way I do today. I also took my language cues from all the music I grew up listening to. Motown and gospel, Queen Latifah, Salt-N-Pepa, Lauryn Hill, Sade. And when I looked around, I saw that this gave me an advantage. The thing I noticed about the existing landscape of speakers was how academic the messages sounded. Eighty percent of the world's population doesn't have a four-year degree, so why would I use academic language if I wanted to appeal to a universal audience? I did, however, understand that music is universal. Everybody wants to hear music. Whitney, Aretha—those women grew up singing in church, and everybody's gonna listen to whatever they're singing, no matter what the message. So I thought about making my presentations more like the experience of hip-hop. I borrowed from Biggie, who was a storyteller. I borrowed from 2Pac, who was a poet. I borrowed from LL's enthusiasm. I borrowed from Salt-N-Pepa's attitude, Public Enemy's Black pride, Lauryn Hill's soulfulness, and Run DMC's trendsetting. I fused all this with what I learned from listening to the speakers I looked up to most—MLK and Malcolm X—and, all together, it made me like nobody else. I became ET, the hip-hop preacher. I made motivational speaking part of popular culture. The way New York rappers made hip-hop universal, I got kids on the block interested in motivational speaking. Later on, CJ, Karl, and I made mixtapes and albums, putting my messages over beats and releasing them the same way a hip-hop artist would.

Sure enough, my following began with young Black men who understood me and felt like they could relate to my experiences. They saw themselves in me. As hip-hop became mainstream and millennials got onto it, they found me, too. When they started climbing up the food chain in corporate America, the white business guys got onto me. And the funniest thing happened: My following shifted. Now just as many white people follow me as Black people. I literally rode the wave of hip-hop into the present moment, because that's the world I knew best. It formed my worldview and my language. It made me, me. And it made me different from everybody else in the business.

I can tell you that I'm successful because I've always felt like an underdog and an outsider. Even though I have money and security and a global following, I just can't take the chip off my shoulder. CJ describes me as the littlest dog on the block, guarding my food as if everybody wanted to eat it. Even though I've quote-unquote "made it," that feeling that I might lose it all or have to go back to where I came from never goes away.

For me, this feeling is fuel. It's an advantage. Outsiders have advantages. First of all, you can see the system from a perspective that nobody else can, which means you can detect its flaws and its weaknesses. The reason corporations bring in outside companies to help fix their own is because an outsider can provide a new, fresh point of view. They can ask questions and make observations without the same bias as someone on the inside. Outsiders and underdogs have the advantage of constant hunger. If you're hungry, it means you can't be satisfied. If you can't be satisfied, you can't get complacent. If you're not complacent, you have a reason to constantly be making progress and constantly be moving forward.

You Are a Businessperson

CJ and LaShanna have always been fearless when it comes to doing business. They'll look someone right in the eye and say, yes, no, and how much. CJ vets everybody who comes through the door, and if they don't pass the smell test, they don't stick around. He has an uncanny ability to sense people's intentions and their willingness to grind. And he's not afraid to tell someone what he thinks of them or to make decisions that carry the weight of the business.

Karl and I, on the other hand, see the business of business and react the same way: We walk in the other direction. When big names and teams started coming to us—Thomas Davis, Joe Dumars, Lawrence Frank, the Detroit Pistons, the Miami Dolphins, the University of Alabama— we were overwhelmed. It was surreal when we started getting invited into locker rooms and hotels and penthouses. We'd walk in and see the spread, the gear, the teams doing Xs and Os, and feel like we were wandering around in a dream. We never imagined ourselves being inside these sacred spaces with this kind of elite company. It was a whole new world. And the business that went along with it felt too big to engage with. I had always been so focused on the psychological and intellectual side of my work that I'd just never considered myself a businessperson. For the entirety of my career, I'd seen myself strictly through a lens of ministry.

I mean this in the philosophical sense of the word. Yes, I was a pastor at a church at the time, but I was focused on ministering to everybody— students, teachers, my audience members, my family, athletes, teams. I was so centered on giving of my gift, that I was missing out on the opportunity to profit from my gift. I looked at money as something that was evil, something that went hand in hand with greed and vanity. As someone who'd deeply internalized Christian faith and the blue-collar mindset, I saw money as a vice, not a virtue.

For the most part, I've never had to worry about business because CJ has always been the businessperson. He's consistently moved forward along that path, eating up knowledge and strategy, steering the ship with confident decisions and decisive action. Because I didn't see myself in those same terms and knew he was taking care of business, I just stayed on my own path of ministry. But at some point, I had to deal with the fact that I was leaving valuable knowledge and skills on the table.

I was being passive about my abilities as a businessperson. In my mind, I thought about wealth in a certain way. Growing up in the African American community, I sometimes thought of or equated rich people with slave owners. If you look at all the money made from railroads, from cotton, from sugarcane, from industry and land that my people built and worked, it can feel strange to want to be a part of the capitalist system that built it. I grew up associating wealth with something bad. In the Bible, there is always a dichotomy of rich and poor—it is harder for a rich man to make it into heaven than for a camel to pass through the eye of a needle.

For so long, I only saw it from one perspective: I had to use my gifts for good and good meant giving. However, I wasn't allowing myself to see how profiting from my gifts could increase my ability to do good on a greater level. CJ put it to me this way: If I wanted to do more good in the world—send kids to school, donate equipment to youth sports programs, buy instruments for music programs, set up summer camps for underprivileged youth—I had to make the money to support that level of giving. By being passive about my potential to do business, I was missing opportunities to advance my ministry.

When I looked back, I could see that I had limited myself to the role of speaker and activist. I had limited myself to developing a select aspect of my career. I was so into the brotherhood part of my life—traveling with Karl and CJ, doing the Mother Teresa thing—that I was not looking at myself as a businessperson. The idea of being passionate, of simply focusing on ministry, was cute, but if I wanted to become more, to earn more, to provide more, I had to shift my paradigm.

Sure, the Bible says that it's difficult for a rich man to make it into heaven, but I made it my aim to redefine what it means to be a rich man. I made it my aim to define what it means to be a Christian businessperson. I could still be competitive, aggressive, demanding, wealthy, *and* be a person of faith, a person of the ministry.

At the time, I was putting two or three kids through college a year, through our foundation, School Days. If I wanted to put fifty kids through college, I had to make more money. I had a nice community church, but if I wanted a real church and a global ministry, I had to make more money. I had substantial savings, but if I wanted to build a legacy for my children, I had to make more money. I had to become a businessperson.

However, the biggest lesson in becoming a better businessperson came about when I refocused on my why. When Dede got sick, I realized that I needed to come up with a plan that didn't rely simply on me talking to crowds of people. I needed a plan that meant I could spend more time taking care of her, as opposed to being on the road constantly. I needed a plan that would make Dede feel more safe and secure than she'd ever been. When I refocused on my why, becoming a

businessperson was the most natural thing to do. Instead of money becoming a vice, it became a form of security.

Today, Dede is healthier than ever. We spend all our time together,
of course. She comes on the road when she can and we live half the year
in California, where the climate is good for her body. Our community
came out for us 120, and took care of us when we needed it most. Dede
is still running things, too. She doesn't know how not to. And we're more
secure than we've ever been. Nothing wrong with that.

Your Gifts Are Your Business

When you think about corporations or brands, you see a product or a
service first. A car. A purse. A shampoo. But if you look behind those
products and services, there were people first: Henry Ford, Louis Vuitton, Johnson & Johnson. A business is the physical manifestation of a
mind and a vision. You can look at a company and see its parking lot and
its building and its desks and its elevators, but all of this is somebody's
thoughts and dreams actualized.

Shifting your mind into business mode means thinking about yourself as a business.

In all the years I saw myself as a minister, I never thought of my gifts
as a way to create products and services. Of course, in some ways, this
was a boon to me—in giving away my gifts, I gained a crazy amount of
intangible value and provided so much for the people who needed it
most. But in order to keep giving of my gifts for the people who need it
most, in order to grow my vision and my impact, I had to shift into the
mind-set of creating products and services as salable value. If you have a

vision, you have a salable product. If you have a salable product, you have a business.

When I realized that I was creating content that people wanted to access, I saw that I could sell this content to corporations and companies who were willing to benefit from my wisdom. I could literally sell my philosophy and ideas to people who wanted to listen to them. I could sell my time and my influence. This book in your hands is the physical manifestation of my philosophy, ideas, time, and influence. When I shifted my mind-set to seeing myself as more than a voice and more than a speaker, I shifted to seeing myself as a businessperson, and today my company is organized by my abilities and philosophies. There's Breathe University, which provides a community and programming for businesses and people trying to understand themselves. There's Game Changers, which helps train fledgling speakers and gives them structure on how to make speaking a career. We've got Make Real Estate Real and Legacy Living, which help people understand the importance of generational wealth—and the idea that wealth isn't just about money and owning property. And, of course, there's Extreme Execution, which is where we help walk people through their Flight Assessment. Had I not started thinking of myself as a businessperson, I might not have understood that I could organize my ideas into arms of a company, which provide different services to different people with different needs.

For those of us who grew up working class, you aren't raised with the idea of seeing yourself as a business. You see yourself as a worker. You see your value in terms of working for somebody else. When you're working class, you decide to give your youth—your twenties and thirties and then some—to somebody else's company. You decide to give your energy and your strength to somebody else's vision. You decide to give your natural gifts to promote somebody else's bottom line. There's nothing wrong with helping somebody else achieve their vision or their goal, as long as it doesn't keep you from achieving your own vision and goal. If you give of yourself without boundaries, you are doing so without clarity about what you want for yourself.

Once you've shifted to see yourself as a business, you need to think practically. Where do you see yourself in business? Which industry? Specifically, what are your gifts and who can benefit from them? What is your product? In which market does your product belong?

Once you've identified some basics, you need to educate yourself. In my case, I had to be willing to ask people for resources. For most of my career, people have come to me, asking me for things they need—a connection, my time, a message—but when I began to think like a businessperson, I started to think about leveraging my relationships and my connections in a different way. I now have enough social and charitable capital that I can ask the people I've helped to help me in return.

The Work

1. What business do you want to be in? What are the challenges of being in that business or starting that business? What are the advantages of being in that business? What resources do you have that you can begin to build your business with?

2. Consider your role in the field. What do you bring to the business? How do your gifts add to the field? How do you see yourself fitting into the field? Conversely, how do you not fit in? What perspective do you bring as an outsider?

3. If you aren't ready to start a business or even if you are, it's important to seek out someone who has gone before you. Find a mentor—alive or in history. Who do you admire in your field? Where did they get their start? What did they read, study, watch? Who was their mentor? What was their path to greatness?

Challenge: What do you want to be—a doctor, a writer, a biologist, a coach? Look at yourself in the mirror and call yourself that thing. Define what that thing means to you. How does this role fit into the business of your life? How does it fit into the business of business? Make a list of the tangible and intangible values it has. Now look at the field you are in. Survey what people are doing and where there is overlap. Now look at what might be missing. Where are there gaps in the field? Look at it from the perspective of an outsider. Make a list of everything that you don't see present in that field and a list of ways your gifts can contribute. Make a list of the people who have been innovators in your field, people who have gone before you and made their mark in the world. List the changes they've made, and put yourself on that list and how you plan to change the game, too.

CHAPTER

10

BUDGET LIVING ON ANY INCOME
BUT YOU OWE YOU MONEY TIME

You Owe You

NOBODY OWES YOU ANYTHING.
BUT YOU OWE YOU EVERYTHING.

What do you want? To get what you want, you have to know what you want. If you don't know what you want, you'll take anything. But if you know what you want, you'll never settle for anything less than that. Once you know what you want, you owe it to yourself to get up every single day and spend the rest of your waking life going after it.

Ask yourself: What do you want out of your life? What do you want in your marriage? What do you want in your career? What do you want from your friendships? What do you want your life to look like? You are the only person responsible for answering these questions and the only person responsible for getting what you want.

At the heart of everything, you are your superpower. You are your gifts. You are your purpose. You are your why. The only reason any of those things exists is because of you. Your dreams are your dreams. Nobody else is going to make your dreams come true except for you. Nobody else owes it to you to make you happy or fulfilled or actualized. The only person who owes you anything is you.

For me, there's comfort in this thought. It means that nobody else is in charge of my future. Nobody else can be held accountable for my happiness. Nobody else is liable for securing my stability or my success or my spiritual fulfillment. The only person who has any responsibility in all of this is me.

Know Thyself

Everything—*everything*—comes from knowing yourself. When you know yourself, you know what you want. When you know yourself, you know what you're working toward. When you know yourself, you know exactly where you're going and what you need to do to get there.

When you look at the most successful businesses, they have a manifesto or a mission statement or a list of values. These places started with a vision. Your value is your identity. It's difficult to be in control of your life or to live the life of your dreams if you don't have an identity. It's easy to get wrapped up in someone else's identity and mission. The people who have identities and values are going to bully you into doing what they value. Very few people who have self-respect and self-love don't have values or identities. The bravest, most confident, have an intimate understanding of themselves; they can't be manipulated because they have an anchor.

We all have obligations in life—caring for people we love, showing up for work and our community—but if you don't know yourself, you can get lost in the obligation itself. You can forget what you want and become entangled with what everybody else wants from you. I know adults who are so consumed with what other people think that they don't realize they have forfeited their entire lives to making other people happy or meeting other people's demands. When you don't know who you are, you look to other people to impress their values and value systems upon you. You look to other people for the blueprint of how to live your life.

In reality, you have to have your own values, your own principles, your own non-negotiables. You owe it to yourself to create your own blueprint. How do you do that?

Make a list of what you believe in. I don't mean just a higher power, but you can include that, too. I mean the things that you wake up every day knowing to be true. For me, I believe in God. I believe in my family. I believe in my church. I believe in my community. I believe in the good of other people. At the end of this list is the most important belief: I believe in myself. It may sound simple, and it may not be true for you today, at this very moment, but you must believe in yourself before you believe in anything else.

Losers focus on winners. Winners focus on winning.

Make a list of your values. These are the things that guide your actions and thoughts every day. I value my relationship with myself. I value my relationships with other people. I value my time alone. I value my body and my mind. I value the support of my community and my family. I value the time and space to work on what I want to work on. At the end of this list is the most important value: I value myself. If I do not value myself, I cannot value anyone or anything else.

Make a list of your non-negotiables. These are the things you are not willing to compromise on, the things that keep your values in place. I know that addiction runs in my family. Because I know that this is part of my DNA, I will not negotiate when it comes to drinking, smoking, gambling, or doing drugs. I just can't risk it. Dede is a non-negotiable. If I'm traveling, I'm traveling with Dede. It's in the contract. If I'm coming, so is she. My quiet time is non-negotiable. When I wake up in the morning, I need time to myself to pray, meditate, and reflect before I share my day with the rest of the world. Your non-negotiables list should be a mirror of your core values and a means of holding fast to your values and your sacred beliefs.

All these lists will begin to create a blueprint for who you are at your core. Of course, your personal experiences and your personality will inform this blueprint, too. For me, the greatest tool in understanding my own personality type has been the Flight Assessment. Before I could see myself within this framework, I was moving through the world with purpose, but I didn't have a good understanding of why I was moving that way. I couldn't yet see how I could move more effectively, how I could work with other people to communicate and be more efficient.

To some people, I look like I'm all over the place—at the church, at schools, in an auditorium, in the locker room, at the prison—but with the Flight Assessment, it becomes clear that this is part of my personality. Most people don't realize that, if they're like me—energetic and intuitive—there is a job and a life path that matches their personality. Many Pilots don't know that they're pilots, and are equipped to make decisions for a team. Many Air Traffic Controllers don't realize how much power they have, and that they're the real leaders of an operation. If you know who you are, you can know what you are, and then see how to apply that to the world. I am a people person, so I go to where the people are.

But even after you've made your blueprint and taken the assessment, there is one more step: You have to want it. Nobody else can want your dreams enough for you to accomplish them. You have to want your dreams. You have to have a focus. You have to want to succeed as bad as you want to breathe. There is no substitute for your own drive and desire. If you don't have that fire, if you don't have that dog, you're not going to accomplish anything. You owe you to have focus. You owe you to have a dream. You owe you to go out there and make it happen.

Make You a Priority

If you're married, your spouse has demands. If you have kids, your kids have demands. If you have a job, your boss has demands. Everybody needs things from you. And that's fine. That's how the world works. But you need things from you, too. And if you don't give yourself what you need, you can't give it to anybody else, either.

The average person has 150 close relationships in their lives. By this calculation, I probably have 300. Now let's say you are attempting to meet the demands of the closest 100 people in your sphere—making a phone call, attending a graduation or a birthday party, buying a gift. You are giving your life over to other people. You are allowing other people to rule the gift of your life. I don't believe you should turn away people in need, but I do believe that you can't be all things to all people. You cannot possibly be taking care of yourself if you are taking care of that many other people.

I know this from experience.

There's something that comes up for many people when they make it out of where they're from and they become successful. I see it with athletes and entrepreneurs who make it out of the hood. It's called survivor's guilt. You feel like you made it through something that other people should have made it through, too—but they didn't and you did. You survived, and you feel bad about it. And to remedy your guilt, you start giving of yourself. You're the only person who went to college and got a good job, so you buy your aunt a car. You help your brother buy a house. You give cash to your cousins and your boy who grew up down the block. You give away everything you have because you're trying to meet the desires of the people who didn't make it to your level of success. There is nothing wrong with generosity, but generosity has its limits before it becomes detrimental to both parties.

I've spoken with NFL and NBA players who feel survivor's guilt so acutely it suffocates their own well-being. But I impress upon them that they have to take care of themselves first so that they can keep performing in their gifts. Because if they can't operate at peak performance, they can't take care of anybody anymore. I also tell them that you may be making any amount of money—$30 mil, $40 mil—but if everybody's coming to you for a handout, you're going to deplete yourself and your legacy. You can't take care of everybody, nor are you responsible for taking care of everybody. I, Eric Thomas, am the sole provider for my family. My mental, emotional, physical, and spiritual health come before anybody else's. I have to put everything into me so that I can continue to provide for my family. I have to take care of myself before I can take care of anybody else.

So often I hear about people giving up their livelihood because they feel that they owe other people before themselves. I talked to a fifty-year-old man the other day who was getting on a plane for the first time. He'd worked his whole life and never made time to go anywhere. Even though he had his tickets booked and was ready to go, he was still uncertain if he should go to the airport and get on the plane. He worried that he wasn't taking care of somebody else by taking care of himself. So often I talk to women who haven't gone back to school or pursued the job they always wanted because they gave it up to raise children. Even as a younger man, I subscribed to the old-fashioned Christian philosophy that a wife should be a man's right-hand helper. I felt that Dede should be helping me with my business as it was growing, but she has always been straight with me. Her dream has always been to be a nurse, and she wasn't letting anybody get in the way of her pursuing that. She was not willing to lose her identity or put aside her dream for my dream. That's deep. It took me some time to understand it, but I take a page from her book now.

My dream isn't anybody else's. My dream is my own and I owe it to myself to pursue it. If I don't pursue it, nobody else will.

There are only twenty-four hours in a day, only 365 days in a year. You don't know how many years you get on this earth. You must live in a way that makes the most of your time here. You owe it to you.

You owe it to you to put yourself first. When you take care of yourself, take the time to see yourself, and get comfortable with being you, only then can you start to take care of other people, see other people, and be comfortable with other people. You can give back when you've given yourself the time to develop and become the focused, centered, actualized person you want to be.

Stop looking for permission to pursue your dreams. They are your dreams. You don't need a cosigner to chase them.

When I started letting go of the expectations the world had of me, I came into a whole new part of Eric Thomas. Closing doors to make room for yourself can be painful—it will be painful. When I left Huntsville for a new life at Michigan State, it was painful. When I left Michigan State to make my own path, it was painful. When I left my church to create a whole new community, it was painful. Growth is painful. Remember when you were a teenager and your bones would ache from a growth spurt? You couldn't get taller, you couldn't become an adult, without going through those spurts. Moving forward is painful. Change is painful. But here's the truth: Staying in the same place is painful, too.

It's just a different kind of pain—one you've gotten used to, like a callus over an old blister. There is no growth without pain. But when you are in touch with yourself, you can check in on yourself and embrace the experience of the growth.

Nobody owes you time but you. You are the only person who will make time for yourself. What does this look like within the reality of life? Start your day by getting centered. Imagine a piece of paper with a dot at the very center. You are the dot. There will be many things that try to move you away from the center, pull you to the edges. Your job every day is to stay as centered and focused as possible. You can't wake up and think, *I need to make this money.* The treasury prints money every day, but they don't print peace or joy or happiness. You can go to Walmart and buy a watch or to Louis Vuitton and buy a purse. But you can't go out and buy your own fulfillment. When you're centered, you can see yourself, you can see where you're supposed to go, you can see your future unfold before you.

For you, getting centered might be meditating. It might mean going for a run. Maybe it's reading the Bible or spending a quiet moment having coffee by yourself. Centering can happen at any time of day, at any moment. It can be while you're on the subway or driving, while you're in your office or walking home from school. Getting centered is about getting your mind right, and your mind is always with you, and you are in charge of your mind.

Think about what your day looks like. Visualize what fulfillment will mean for you today. Paint a picture of the ideal day. And if you're not there yet, if you can't have your ideal day yet, think about what today needs to look like to get to that ideal day next week, next month, next year. Think about what your week looks like. What do you need to do to get to the next level? What does your month look like? Your year? Make a plan to get yourself on track. Nobody is going to make your plans but you. And you owe it to yourself to be the center of your own plan.

If you're willing to put in the blood, sweat, and tears, you can have, be, and do what you want.

Part of making yourself a priority is spending time alone. When you need to figure out your superpower, you spend time alone. When you search for your purpose, you spend time alone. When you connect to your why, you spend time alone. Knowing yourself requires you to be okay with being alone. You cannot be afraid of missing out. You must push aside the fear of rejection. You must be okay with being on the outside. Being on the outside gives you perspective. It allows you to see yourself better—to see what you need to move forward. When you know yourself, you get comfortable with being alone, with loving yourself enough to spend time with you. You stop fearing what other people think, what the institutions want, what the systems need. You can see yourself outside of them and in your own fullness. And, sure enough, when you get comfortable with you, you begin to attract opportunities and other people. Nobody will embrace being with you unless you can embrace being with you.

When you have a blueprint—your values, your beliefs, your focus, your self-knowledge—then you must set a standard. You owe it to yourself to constantly evaluate your own performance and the way you spend your time. Goals are good, but standards will get you to the next level. Time management within those standards will create a natural flow for meeting those standards. I ask myself, *Did I do what I set out to do when I started my day?* I ask myself if my time was used in the ways that make me happiest. I have plenty of opportunities at this point in my life— people ask me to do talk shows, offer me TV shows, invite me to Hollywood, and on private planes. But I have to hold me accountable for my time. And not every opportunity will meet my standards for how to spend that time. I can't visit all the schools and churches and prisons I want to if I'm on somebody else's joyride. I can't spend time with my family and my kids if I'm running off to do somebody else's job. I owe it to me to be accountable to my standards. So, ask yourself every day: *Did you use your time the way you wanted to? Did you worship? Did you exercise? Did you meditate? Did you spend time with the people you wanted to—your family, your friends, your community? When you spent your time, were you present? Did you live fully in the moment? Were you focused on the relationships you want to be in and build?*

Your Life Is Your Legacy

My mom always says that every generation should give back. By this she means to look to the generation before you and see what they did, and then do your part to further their work. My great-grandparents moved their families from the Jim Crow South to the North in search of opportunity. My grandparents worked any kind of job they could so their children might have more than they did. My parents moved out of the projects and got stable jobs in industry so that I might have more than they did. We didn't go to Disney or Mexico, but we had three square meals and clothes and traveled a little here and there. Dede and I were the first generation of our families to complete a college education. We had children only when we had stable lives and jobs. Our children grew up in a two-parent household. And today my kids have real opportunity. They went to the best schools and have connections I could only dream about. My son Jalin works with NBA teams and my daughter Jayda has a master's in psychology. Of course, now they worry about the privileges they've grown up with, but that in itself is a privilege.

If you want to have a legacy, you need to be the standard bearer of your generation. You need to set a standard that will help to further the next generation. This is not just about financial stability. So often, we think of generational wealth as simply financial. But generational wealth is emotional and mental and spiritual. We inherit much more than money. We inherit a way of life. I created a legacy by committing to myself and my standards.

Now is the time to begin building your legacy. Now is the time to take control. Now is the time to do the work. Now is the time to dream of what greatness lies ahead. But not only to dream—to become your dream. To *become* great. The time has come to take hold of your life. The time has come to step into yourself. To begin living life the way that only you can live it. The time has come to become you. The time has come to put this book down. The time has come to go write the book of you.

ACKNOWLEDGMENTS

I am truly humbled by every encounter, every conversation, every hand-shake, every encouraging word from everyone I meet—in my church, on the street, at special events. You are the reason I do what I do. Thank you.

Thank you to the team at Harmony/Rodale, including our editor, Matthew Benjamin, for taking our work from self-published to the big leagues. To Leslie Pariseau for taking this journey with me.

Thank you to Les Brown, Bob Proctor, Tony Nuckolls, Bill Emerson, Dan Gilbert, Thomas Davis, Chris Paul, Reggie Bush, Tyrese Gibson, Glenn Twiddle, Incipio Academy, Stephen Tulloch, Sean "Diddy" Combs, Victor Oladipo, Cam Newton, Demario Davis, Michael B. Jordan, Giavanni Ruffin, Omarion, Kaleb Thornhill, Brian Bostick, Isaiah Thomas, BJ Stabler, June Archer, Anthony "Showtime" Pettis, Kenneth Nelson, Duke Roufus, Prince and Chanel Fielder, Lawrence Frank, Marc Jackson, Geoffrey Schmidt, Niya Butts, Mark Dantonio, Mike Davis, Scott Drew, and Alvin Brooks III and the team at Baylor, Drew

ACKNOWLEDGMENTS

Valentine and the team at Loyola, Disclosure, Mikestro, Ashley Iserhoff, Tom Izzo, Buffini & Company, Kyani, Vondale Singleton, the Oakwood legends who inspired me: Dennis Ross III, Virtue (mad love for the Trotter sisters) and Shavon Floyd, Sharon Riley and Faith Chorale, Angelique Clay, Angela Brown, Brian McKnight, W. S. B. (Willing Succeeding and Black), DP (Owen Simmons), Voices of Triumph (Damien Chandler), Wintley Phipps, Barry Black, Chris Willis, Take 6, Duawne Starling, Paul and Patrick Graham ("The Twins"), Bell Tower Ministries, Irvin Daphnis, Melvyn Hayden, Quincy Harris, Steven Tullock, and ConnectFive.

Thank you to everybody I've worked with at New Balance Athletic Shoes Inc., Under Armour Inc., ESPN, NBC, Quicken Loans, and Shaun Harris with AT&T.

Ladies of my life: Grandma Gwen, Grandma Lama, Auntie Wanda, Auntie Cleo, Auntie Booby, and Auntie Tawana, for your continued support since diapers. Plus, Sister Lamb, Ma Trotter, and Ma Bez (Sterling Foster).

Men of my life: Uncle Bruce, Uncle Jimmy, Uncle David, Tim and Wayne Smith, Robert King, Leon Burnette, Pastor James Doggette, Pastor T. Marshall Kelly, Preston Turner, Rupert Cannonier, Carlas Quinney Sr., Coach Daniel Bogan, Jerald Clift Kyle, Renee Chandler, Pastor James Black, Elder Eric Calvin Ward, Pastor Sean Holland, Pastor Larry Trice, Pastor Nathan Dixon, Steven Coffey, Pastor Walter Gibson, Hope Fellowship and E. E. Cleveland . . . accountability.

Brothers: LaDon Daniels, Lee Lamb, Lloyd Paul (shout-out to St. Marteen), Carlas Quinney, Burks Hollands, Charles Arrington, Shannon Austin, Greg Arneaud, Adrian Marsh, John Samon, Derrick Green, Quest Green, Joey Kibble, Jamie Cook, Inky Johnson, Jeremy Anderson, and Karl Phillips.

Thank you to all of my support systems. I couldn't possibly name everyone, but among the many are the Quinney family, the Tyus family, LaShanna Fountain, J. D., the Arrington family, Walter Bivens, Derrick Williams, my A Place of Change Ministry family, Rodney Patterson, Murray Edwards, Dr. Lee June, Dr. Bonita Curry, Dr. Sonja Gunnings, Dr. Pero Dagbovie, Brandon Bostick, LBJ, Meek Mill, the Lamb family, Tobe and Fat Nwigwe, Nell Grant, Lamar Higgins, Mostafa Ghonim, Jeff Idehen, Jemal King, Josh Hatch, Derek Bowe, Tony Biancosino, Anthony Flynn, Dorothy L. Green, and the Austin family. I appreciate all of you, and everyone mentioned in this book.

Gone but not forgotten: Uncle Mike, Uncle Ben, Allen Johnson, Kay Craig-Harper, Renee Braxton, Renia Braxton, Glenda Craig-Anderson, Elder Ward, Elder Cleveland, MaBez, Chris Daniels, and Pastor P. C. Willis.

Thank you, Mom, and the rest of my family for believing in me.

The ETA Squad: CJ, Karl, Elle "L," Tiffany Hayes, Kamela Quinney, Ashante Tucker, Valerie Hawkins, Nicky Saunders, Cierra Pryor, Marshall Fox, Dr. Cheryl McBride Brown, Train Quinney, VaLarie Humphrey, Charles Terry, Brandon Burns, Shelly Vaughn, and Jose Bennett. I know that I have the most talented team in the business, and I'm so excited about our future together.

Thank you to all my YouTube, Twitter, Instagram, and Facebook supporters and everyone who has ever purchased a book or an MP3, worn a T-shirt, downloaded the mixtape, forwarded a video, and or told someone about me and my work. Because of you, I get to wake up every morning and do what I was created to do.

To my wife, Dilsey "Dede" Moseley, thank you for being my best friend, rock, and unyielding accountability partner. You push me to be

ACKNOWLEDGMENTS

the best, and that makes me want to give you the best. You, Jalin, and Jayda—the twin joys of my life—it is my privilege to be your father. It doesn't get any better.

Last and always, I give honor to God, who shows me every day that impossible is nothing.

And special thanks to my haters for pushing me to greatness. Continued blessings on you and your family from henceforth and forevermore. —Matthew 5:44

Grateful,
ET

ABOUT THE AUTHOR

ERIC THOMAS has reached millions with his story about going from homeless to becoming one of the world's top motivational speakers. He has been profiled in *GQ* and *Sports Illustrated* and on *ESPN*. He has worked with corporate teams at Nike, Under Armour, AT&T, Quicken Loans, Procter & Gamble, UPS, and more. Every year, he works with the NFL, the NBA, and the NCAA, as well as dozens of individual teams and players across the country throughout their respective seasons. He has a BA in education from Oakwood College, an HBCU in Oakwood, Alabama, and a master's and a PhD in education from Michigan State. He lives in Lansing, Michigan, and San Diego, California, with his wife, Dede.

Go to ETYouOweYou.com to learn more and to access the *You Owe You* workbook, designed to help you explore and practically apply each value and principle identified here.